DO YOU KNOW . . .

- The five different kinds of problem bosses and how to make each work for you?
- How to go over your boss's head and gain authority in your company—*without* being fired?
- How to make even a hostile boss take a personal interest in your career success?
- How to dominate your boss *and make him or her thank you for it?*
- How to ax your boss and become your own supervisor?

Every employee, sooner or later, is forced to deal with "the boss from hell." But the smart ones know how to turn a liability into an advantage. This book will show you how to wrestle control of your job, your career and your life from the person above you and put it back where it belongs—in your own hands!

HOW TO FIRE YOUR BOSS

CHRIS MALBURG

BERKLEY BOOKS, NEW YORK

Grateful acknowledgment is made for permission to reprint from the following copyrighted material:

Do It My Way or You're Fired by David W. Ewing, copyright © 1983 by David W. Ewing. Reprinted by permission of John Wiley & Sons, Inc. All Rights Reserved. Published simultaneously in Canada.

The Executive Dilemma by Eliza Collins, articles copyright © by President and Fellows of Harvard College; all other materials copyright © 1985 by John Wiley & Sons, Inc. Reprinted by permission of John Wiley & Sons, Inc. All Rights Reserved.

One-on-One With Andy Grove by Andrew S. Grove, copyright © 1987 by Andrew S. Grove. Reprinted by permission of G. P. Putnam's Sons. All rights reserved.

HOW TO FIRE YOUR BOSS

A Berkley Book / published by arrangement with
the author

PRINTING HISTORY
Berkley edition / May 1991

ISBN: 0-425-12734-6

A BERKLEY BOOK ® TM 757,375
Berkley Books are published by The Berkley Publishing Group,
200 Madison Avenue, New York, New York 10016.
The name "BERKLEY" and the "B" logo
are trademarks belonging to Berkley Publishing Corporation.

PRINTED IN THE UNITED STATES OF AMERICA

10 9 8 7 6 5 4 3 2 1

There are two people I wish to acknowledge who were instrumental in the development of this material and support of this effort:

Marilyn: The only woman I know who makes a fabulous living, does her own nails, and cooks! If you don't know where you stand with Marilyn, you just aren't listening!

Kenny: One of the finest people I've had the pleasure of working for, and someone who knew when to let go.

Contents

Introduction

Most of us have endured the agony of a boss who rumbles over our careers like a runaway steamroller. If you have even a few years' experience in the work force, chances are you have thought about what you could do to protect your career from the abuses of an incompetent supervisor. It may have occurred to you that getting rid of your boss's influence could greatly benefit your upward mobility.

It did for me. Beginning with graduation from college and for the first ten years of my career, I was "blessed" with every one of the obdurate bosses described in this book. You might say that I've learned how not to manage people from some of the best of the worst. Many of the examples I've related come from my own experiences both as an employee and as a consultant. Has your boss ever stolen an idea from you and passed it off as his or her own? Mine have, and it's not fun. Does your boss have such a dogmatic, overbearing demeanor (emphasis on *mean*) that no one can voice an innovative idea without being first stripped of all dignity, then embarrassed to death, and finally paraded before the world? How about the boss whose frail standing in the company causes his endorsement on raises and promotions to become the proverbial kiss of death? My experience with just such a boss caused me to finally fire him and seize control of my own career. That experience, along with the close-range observation of hundreds of bosses who were my clients, inspired the formula for firing your boss shown in this book.

If you face any of the bosses I've described and are looking for a way out, this must be one of the most unnerving times in your career. It was for me. I have used the methods described in this book to fire my own bosses. These methods continue to work for me every day as a management consultant, and they can be just as successful for you. Don't suffer in silence one minute longer. Read the book and use the techniques. The light at the end of the tunnel defined by a solid course of action to make things better will cause your anxiety level to drop immediately. Your ability to deal with a problem boss will improve dramatically. Once you recognize your boss's shortcomings, you've won the war. Problems that may have been placed at your feet before can now be traced to their real cause—often the boss. Finally, your unique situation can be used to get the ultimate results you are looking for.

What does it mean to fire your boss? First, it does not mean GETTING your boss fired. Most incompetent managers can accomplish that with no help from you. People who successfully fire their bosses see a positive change in their own management style. When you remove your boss from your career you gain control over supervision, your approach to assignments, and the goal/reward structure of your job. You develop a rich appreciation for risk taking, a tolerance for new ideas, and respect for capable superiors and subordinates. You develop greater independence and a sense of balance between supervision, authority, and responsibility. Firing your boss allows you to control the progression of your career without interference and hindrance from a boss who may be ill-equipped to help you. Firing the boss establishes your credentials as someone with energy and initiative, someone willing to take responsibility—a self-starter.

Much has been written by management theorists about directing subordinates and the traits that make an effective leader. There has been little discussion, however, of what today's generation of workers require from their leaders. David W. Ewing, in his book *Do It My Way or You're Fired* (John Wiley and Sons, New York, NY 1983), was one of the first to recognize the employee's bill of rights. Ewing states that subordinates are entitled to:

(*a*) Competent management
(*b*) Loyalty
(*c*) Moral practices
(*d*) Commitment to employees and their needs
(*e*) Freedom from unnecessary intrusion and oppressive regulation.

Surprisingly few people, bosses included, know what it means to be effectively managed. According to Andrew Grove in his book *One-on-One With Andy Grove*, (G.P. Putnam's Sons, New York, NY) it means "getting the time and attention of a knowledgeable person who is paid to provide it. Getting trained in the rudiments of the job. Getting coaching and evaluation. Getting encouragement when you are bogged down and a kick in the ass when you need it. Having someone to talk to, whether about a machine failure or about your career."

To this I add that a qualified boss:

(*a*) Keeps subordinates informed of developments in the firm that could affect their work or careers

(b) Eliminates duplication of work and snags in the work flow

(c) Anticipates problems in the work flow and solves them before they affect subordinates

(d) Creates an environment where constructive criticism flows in BOTH directions

(e) Sets precise goals and gives feedback on how these goals are being met

(f) Varies his management style to suit the situation.

If you have difficulty finding these traits in your boss, chances are he or she will hinder your career development. Your course of action includes staying under the boss's incompetent tutelage and hoping for the best; leaving the job; or firing the boss and taking charge of your own career. Working for a buffoon places your career advancement in serious jeopardy, not to mention your personal well-being if you work for one of the extreme boss types described later. Fleeing to a new job may help only until you meet your next incompetent boss. Firing your boss, on the other hand, places you in control of your future, not just for today, but for the long haul. It does not require leaving your job.

No longer will modern employees accept a boss who does not provide the leadership they need. Today's employees are creative and independent. They know as much or more about their jobs as their bosses do. They demand participation in every phase of their work. The work environment of the nineties assumes that subordinates know their jobs and will insist that the boss act as a guide, adviser, and planner, rather than a specialist at harassment.

A word about the gender used in this book. I have labored to make this book as nonsexist as possible. Since women have come into their own in the work force, incompetence has become an equal-opportunity malady. Problems female bosses present are no different from those of their male counterparts—they can ruin your career just as effectively.

• • •

Together we will explore ways to equip ourselves against bosses who would annihilate our careers in order to help their own. Take my hand and hold on tight. The catacombs of corporate America are a cold and slippery place where all breeds of lumbering maladroit bosses roam.

> Chris Malburg
> April 1990
> Palos Verdes Estates, CA

I

Pigeonhole Your Boss: Classifying Bosses and Potential Problems

Just as bosses come in all shapes and sizes, so do their management styles and the problems each presents to our jobs and careers.

As a management consultant I get to see the turmoil that bosses in all sorts of different industries create. Industries that employ highly paid professionals such as medical, legal, accounting, and brokerage all seem to suffer from a "prima donna syndrome." I've seen a securities broker fire a subordinate who really needed his job for accidentally removing a pencil (yes, an ordinary yellow number two lead pencil!) from his boss's desk. The boss's rationale was, How can he service his clients if he has to spend his valuable time searching for pencils? Besides, if the employee stole a pencil there's no telling where his life of crime would stop. Prima donna professionals think that no one matters but them. They believe that simple human kindness, like saying please and thank you, should take a backseat to the paycheck.

Manufacturing industries seem to have bosses who treat subordinates as an extension of the assembly line. They refuse to recognize a worker's ambitions, need for creativity, ideas, and desire for job enrichment. I have heard just such a boss say, "If your idea was worth a damn, don't you think I would have already thought of it? Now, get back to work and stop wasting my time!"

Service industries appear to employ more managers with split personalities. The nice side appears in public before the customer. Employees get to see the darker side. These are the bosses who employ a tone that's as smooth as silk while someone who "counts" is within earshot, but then go on a screaming rampage as soon as that person leaves.

Whatever your industry, we've all seen horrible bosses before. Chances are you probably work for one of these boss types:

Lyan Lobby, the politician, who says, "I appreciate your input and you've fingered several valid points. But what about the fallout from Department X? They can make life miserable for me. We'd better water down your proposal."

Letsall Getalong, the pleaser, who says, "The executive committee denied your raise. It wasn't the right time. They didn't want to hear about your work on X, Y, or Z. I'll make it up to you in your salary review next year. Don't you trust me?"

Imagonna Grabontoitz, the disorganized incompetent, who says, "The officer's meeting started without me. When I got there, time was short, so I didn't get past the first paragraph in presenting your idea before Blabbermeister cut me off and they moved on to janitorial expenses."

Princess Rising Star, the juvenile boss, who says, "We'll do it my way because I'm the boss and I say so."

I. B. Meantuu, the locomotive boss, who says, "Don't give me any silly-assed bullshit about how you think this should be done. I've forgotten more about widgets than you'll ever know."

Most problem bosses fall into one or more of these five

categories. Some cross between these types to form hybrids. Still others are like a chameleon, one type one day and another the next, whatever fits the occasion but always to your detriment. The five boss types above must be recognized for the villainous cretins they are. Firing your boss first demands that you recognize the type of boss with which you are dealing. Just as techniques vary from driving a race car to driving the family station wagon, so do the methods of dealing with various boss types. In this chapter we will identify the difference between the five major boss categories and learn how to deal with the peculiarities of each.

THE POLITICIAN

Political bosses are acutely aware of the environment around them. They play office politics to the detriment of their own jobs as well as those of their subordinates. Rather than letting their work speak for itself, these demagogues rely on a series of "old boy networks," promises, and quid pro quo (return favors) to get the job done. To be sure, such things figure in most work environments. Political bosses, however, think they cannot make it on the merits of their own work and must rely on the push they get from politics. Political relationships can take your boss only so far. Beyond that point, there must be genuine ability. The fact remains that talent can beat political relationships any day.

Observe your political boss. He or she probably insists on being the sole spokesperson for the department. Subordinates are seldom allowed to appear at interdepartmental meetings or to reduce the stranglehold the politician has on his little fiefdom. This treacherous lout takes credit for all the work that comes out of his department. He ensures that credit for success is attributed to his skill as a supervisor.

Likewise, any problems are passed off as "the folks' inability to work as independently as he would like."

Usually the politician will not allow you to be noticed by anyone else in the company. Lyan Lobby insists on acting as the sole judge and jury of your work. Your promotion and raises are entirely at his discretion. Lobby often judges a subordinate's value by political factors such as their connections within the company or the school they attended, rather than their talent.

On the other side of the coin, bosses who are oblivious to or unskilled at office politics are equally as dangerous as the "good ol' boy" political wag. Working for a boss out of the political mainstream of the company can place you in the same predicament simply by association. Such a boss has less likelihood of gaining solid support for the needs of his or her department. The work and the ideas that come from this boss and his department are viewed with mistrust.

Your boss must not be allowed to diminish the quality of your work. You will have to labor doubly hard just to overcome the negative stigma transmitted by a boss who fails to earn the confidence of the powers that be. Understand that the way the company views your work depends to a great degree on the status of your boss.

Identify the Politician

If politicians looked and acted like their stereotypes the job of identification would be easy. Political bosses, however, are usually smooth talking and sometimes even well liked within the company. If you look closely, though, you will see that politicians have an obsessive concern with how people perceive their actions and motivations. The politician lives life as if treading on eggshells. Seemingly inconsequential events are extremely important to the political hack.

If your boss refuses to allow anyone to present an idea as his or her own, you may be dealing with a politician as well as a megalomaniac. To the politician, information equals power. He will keep as much knowledge to himself as possible. This tendency parallels the juvenile boss who views himself as the glue that holds the group together.

Watch for back stabbing by the politician. Politicians have the ability to make you think they are in your corner when the facts prove otherwise. Bosses who speak ill of others behind their backs are playing politics. You could be the next one at whom he or she takes a whack.

I once saw a situation where a politician, Dewey Cheatem, was called on the carpet for budget overruns. Being adept at his craft, Cheatem deftly shifted the blame to a subordinate in another department. He even solicited (and got) the help of the subordinate's immediate boss who himself was a dupe and could not politically afford to oppose Cheatem. The coconspirators did not anticipate, however, that the subordinate had documentation that Cheatem spent ninety-five percent of the project's budget gallivanting around the country on a trip that not only did not contribute to the effort but that was never budgeted for in the first place. When the subordinate went over Cheatem's head to try to clear his reputation, he was told that these things happen and for his own good he should let it slide. He lost. Eventually he left the company in frustration. A postscript to this story: Cheatem was later sent off to northern Michigan (his firm's equivalent of corporate Siberia), where it gets so cold he was seen with his hands in his own pockets!

Observe how your boss supports both you and the rest of the staff. Politicians are fair-weather friends at best. The worst will cast you adrift in the political soup at the first hint of trouble. Politicos will distance themselves from people for no reason other than their apparent political status.

What to Do

Political winds blow hot and cold. Your career may temporarily (and artificially) prosper while working for a boss on the way up the political ladder. Your fortunes will plummet even faster, however, and for reasons beyond your control when the boss inevitably falls from grace. Beware the ancient canon that says "no one will step on you faster when you fall than those on whom you trod to rise."

Maintain a safe distance from the politician. Frequently, he may try to draw you into the political fray. Resist the temptation. Let him fight his own political wars so that when the ice cracks and he falls through, you are not dragged down as well.

Bosses whose political fortunes have faltered risk losing their jobs. Often the company will ask if it really needs the problem boss. The answer may be no. Find a lifeboat and bolt from a political boss on a sinking ship. This may come in the form of interdepartmental transfers. Choose the target department carefully so that you don't jump back into the abyss from which you just escaped. Also beware of the possibility that the new boss, perhaps a politician, too, may be hiring you as a form of one-up-manship.

I once knew of a boss who strove to create an image of himself as the hardest-working employee in the company. To perpetuate this illusion, he even answered his phone in an out-of-breath, harried voice. Before leaving the office each day he made sure that his boss had already left. If he worked as hard at his job as he did at office politics he would have been a superstar. Alas, he didn't and he wasn't. This guy was so paranoid that he probably thought the conference on the pitcher's mound at baseball games was about him! Soon his paranoia at being one-upped extended to going through people's trash cans (the smart ones locked their offices and desks at night) to see what information might be gleaned. Upper management was astute enough to recognize this individual for what he was: a political hack. He was never promoted. His department became a swinging door where only the naive wanted in. The firm lost many promising people who became fed up with the world of office politics dictated by the boss. These people could not find a way to distance themselves and break the stranglehold he had on their careers. Their only way out was to leave the company. They were needlessly beaten by the political boss.

Here are the ways to identify a politician, some hazards to watch out for, and different approaches to gain control:

POLITICAL BOSS

Identifying Characteristics	*Hazards to Watch For*
1. Smooth-talking salesman type, glad-hander	1. Gives little support when you need it the most
2. Obsessed with others' impressions of their actions and motivations	2. Won't give you credit when deserved
3. Megalomaniac. Seizes credit for others' work	3. Afraid to oppose a more politically powerful adversary
4. Information junkie. Believes that information equals power	4. Calculating and a user of people

5. Speaks ill of others
   behind their backs
6. Fair-weather friend.
   Likely to jump ship
7. Prone to
   demagoguery
8. Paranoid of others
   plotting against
   him/her

> *Approach to Gain Control*
> 1. Distance yourself from him/her.
> 2. Don't fight his/her political
>   battles.
> 3. Jump ship if necessary.

THE PLEASER BOSS

It's amazing how slippery the pleaser can be. He or she can foul your career as easily as the politician. This boss will say almost anything to anyone to avoid a confrontation. The pleaser replaces the brutal truth with platitudes that sound nice but mean little. He relies on everyone's tendency to avoid unpleasant realities. Unlike the politician, who knows that his cunning will achieve a long-term goal, the pleaser simply wants to roll along with the status quo.

The pleaser carries the banner of the corporate worm. Where the politician savors the intricacies of corporate infighting, the pleaser stays well away from the melee. Most pleasers bear the bruises of many lost corporate scuffles. As a wounded veteran, the pleaser loathes any more confrontation than the job requires. Pleasers such as Letsall Getalong see themselves as passive conduits of information. Getalong's boss tells him what to do and he in turn tells the subordinates. He does little to cause workers to be more productive or produce higher-quality work.

This becomes dangerous when the worm weakens at a time when your boss needs to be at his most tenacious. If the pleaser asks, "Don't you trust me?" the answer is NO!! NEVER. NOT IN A MILLION YEARS.

One particular Letsall Getalong had the backbone of a marshmallow. His subordinates said it was nice working for him. He said nice things. Never raised his voice. Took his people to lunch. Tried to give them pleasant pep talks. But . . . Letsall had no status in the company. When challenged by his own boss, he would back down (all the while saying nice things so as not to offend). He was not respected. Getalong failed to develop his part of the business. As a result of his ineptitude, not one of his subordinates rose to prominence under his leadership. Worse, his people were tainted by being associated with him.

Getalong's mushiness was exposed when he was forced by his boss to hire someone (Lyan Lobby) over several of his own subordinates to head a new department. Knowing the rift this would cause among the group, Letsall took the typical worm's way out: He lied.

Without a word, Lobby appeared one Monday morning and was introduced as a peer. Strike one. Lobby was also paid thirty percent more than anyone else, a fact that inevitably found its way into the company grapevine. Strike two. Getalong never told the rest of the staff that Lobby's position was higher than theirs. Lobby soon made it clear to all that he was the heir apparent to the new department head position. Strike three. Not only was Lobby ostracized by a staff that was soon bound tightly against him, his adverse notoriety soon made both he and Getalong laughingstocks throughout the company. The political machine cranked against them both. Lobby accomplished nothing and was fired. Getalong's subordinates left the firm in revulsion. Letsall himself lost all credibility and was eventually forced out.

Identify the Pleaser

Pleasers are easy to spot. Since most pleasers are veterans of lost company battles, they are usually well seasoned. The pleaser regards innovation as too risky. When presented with a novel idea, the pleaser will say all the right things to feign interest, then make a beeline for the door. If forced to act on an innovative concept, the pleaser will characteristically seek refuge by going through the "proper channels" (a corporate euphemism for shifting responsibility).

Pleasers are stagnant in their careers. They have landed in a comfortable pond and are waiting until retirement. You cannot hitch your rising star to a pleaser and expect to go anywhere fast.

Pleasers can be spotted by their reluctance to assert authority. Because they fear using their power, pleasers cannot be trusted to lead effectively. Additionally, they see themselves as peacemakers, seeking compromise between adverse parties. Outright war does not produce positive results. But constructive disagreements produce challenges to improve. This secures a healthy work environment. The pleaser, however, views any disagreement as unpleasant and will attempt to stop it immediately. The movers and shakers of the company do not respect the pleaser. The political bosses have nothing to fear from the pleaser and will ignore him.

What to Do

The pleaser thrives on approval and recognition. Therefore, use this to your advantage and manage the pleaser. Let the pleaser know when he does something to your liking. If he knows what you like and that he will gain your favorable recognition by doing those things, he will be more likely to behave well toward you. Communication with the pleaser must be straightforward and honest. If authority, greater autonomy, or new projects will make you happy, be sure to let the pleaser know.

Similarly, let the pleaser know what behaviors you will not tolerate. By doing this, you capitalize on his or her built-in tendency to follow the path of least resistance.

Stay away from an opposing relationship with the pleaser. If he views you as someone difficult to get along with, he may stop trying to please you and just stay away.

Once you've told him or her what you need, maintain the pressure. Remember, this boss has a natural tendency to sweep the issues under the rug and to not act on things that could cause conflict. Without being a whiner, let the worm/boss know that he has the power to make you a happy camper.

Just as pleasers want you to be happy, they want their own bosses to be even happier. Therefore, produce results that will please their bosses and reflect positively on you. Companies that have interdepartmental meetings (such as sales or planning) provide an excellent opportunity for this. If giving a group presentation, use an example of an occasion where your worm/boss was not present and you successfully carried the ball. Tell the boss how much you learned by being in charge, even if only temporarily.

Most pleaser bosses are not well regarded throughout the organization. They simply do not get good results. Therefore, you must distance yourself from your worm/boss as much as possible. Get to know the boss's boss. This individual can positively influence your career and must be made aware of your abilities. Eventually you may receive an assignment directly from the boss's boss. Good for you.

You have successfully placed a barrier, however small, between you and the worm. Continue to keep the worm informed of what you are doing, how long your assignment will take, and what impact, if any, it will have on your other work. To do otherwise will likely make your boss insecure and could work against you after the project ends.

Lastly, make sure the pleaser doesn't just agree with you to mollify you. If discussions with your boss are pleasant but get nothing done, he has buffaloed you just like everyone else. Get the straight scoop. Find out if the boss has taken any action to make you a happy and effective worker. If he has failed to act, confront him and let him know that you mean business. The pleaser boss will disappoint someone who won't say a word before someone he knows to be vocal about his displeasure.

Here are the ways to identify a pleaser, some hazards to watch out for, and different approaches to gain control:

PLEASER BOSS

Identifying Characteristics	Hazards to Watch For
1. Avoids criticizing even when deserved	1. Deludes you into thinking you have no problems when you may
2. Nice to work for, nice person	2. You can become tainted by being associated with him.
3. Avoids innovation and most risks	3. Impossible to make a name for yourself

4. Avoids confrontation; a real wimp
5. Not above lying to save himself
6. Stagnant career; marking time, parked in his/her job
7. Uses the role of arbitrator and peacemaker
8. Not respected among peers

4. Your upward mobility is stifled.

Approach to Gain Control

1. Tell him/her what you want.
2. Let him know when he does something right.
3. Make him/her your friend, not your adversary.
4. Please his/her boss.
5. Gain recognition outside of the pleaser's department.
6. Distance yourself from the pleaser.

THE DISORGANIZED INCOMPETENT

Disorganization indicates inferior productivity and capability. Your boss's incompetence may be caused by disorganization, or his disorganization may be due to incompetence. Though less likely, the possibility exists that disorganization effectively masks your boss's true genius.

Whatever the cause, bosses who are disorganized, incompetent, or both must be dealt with before they bring you down.

Such bosses unfavorably impact most everyone with whom they come in contact. Disorganization makes even the most productive people less effective. Disorganization creates tasks that are not given in the best sequence to the most qualified people. Disorganization and incompetence usually combine to produce needlessly short deadlines. Mistakes most often occur under undue time pressure. Guess who gets blamed. Certainly not the DI (disorganized, incompetent) boss. By this stage of his or her career he or she has become adept at finding a scapegoat.

Some DI bosses cultivate the image of an absent-minded professor to such a degree that people make allowances for them. I knew of one such boss who developed disorganized streams of serpentine reasoning to such an art that he was actually rewarded with a promotion. His boss told me, "I don't have the slightest idea what Grabontoitz is usually talking about. If his reasoning is so far over my head that I can't understand him, he must be brilliant." Unfortunately for Grabontoitz's subordinates, the truth was all too clear.

Do not react to a disorganized, incompetent boss by pointing out his shortfalls. Remember you are not the boss and such behavior is unseemly. Rubbing the DI's nose in your own abilities won't mean much to someone with so little regard for perfection anyway. Besides, there are other, more effective ways to use this type of boss to your own advantage. In fact, the DI boss presents a cornucopia of potential opportunities.

Identify the Disorganized Incompetent

Observe the wake made by the DI boss. You will see a turbulent ocean of cancelled meetings and excessive overtime costs. Such a boss subscribes to the notion that a clean desk is the sign of a sick mind. Because of his or her inability to focus on the goal and steps required to get there, the DI boss plays catch-up. He or she always juggles several things at once. This does not seem unusual. Most of us juggle several responsibilities associated with our jobs and personal lives at the same time. The problem comes when your DI boss passes what you thought was the apple he was juggling to you and it turns out to be a double-edged sword with no handle.

You can usually spot DI bosses by their inability to manage time. They are always in a hurry. These are the people who DON'T set their watches ahead of the real time to compensate for their tardiness. Because they are late, they make others late. Business runs on a schedule. For busy people, punctuality translates to respect for others' time as well as your own. DI bosses show little regard for either their time or anyone else's.

When asked about missed deadlines, the DI boss will often cite an unreasonable time frame or conjure up a point that was omitted from the original assignment. He or she misuses the saying that there is always time to do it again but never time to do it right.

The disorganized, incompetent boss shoots from the hip. Rather than taking time to research an answer, he will take a shot in the dark and hope for the best. The DI boss expresses such prognostications with qualifiers such as "preliminarily," "it would seem to me," "on the surface," etc. His or her subordinates are left to explain what he really meant. This has been true even of recent United States presidents who shot from the hip on questions from the press, only to be criticized later when research proved the president's facts to be wrong.

The disorganized incompetent does not prepare a plan of attack for most tasks. In fact, to him or her, preparation of such a plan wastes valuable time. "Why plan? It only gets in the way of what would have happened anyway," says the DI, Imagonna Grabontoitz.

Observe how Grabontoitz interacts with his peers and superiors. He observes only the barest of social protocol. Without even realizing, he makes social gaffs. His peers generally do not hold him in high regard, mostly due to his disorganization and inability to become absorbed into the social culture of the firm.

Woe be to those who have a DI boss. These are not congenial people like the pleaser. They don't have time for social amenities. Disorganization causes the DI to be always under the gun. This pressure-cooker atmosphere creates a taskmaster approach to management rather than one of participation. The DI runs his or her shop on the principles of management by crisis. The DI's crisis quickly becomes that of the subordinates.

The DI boss works extremely long hours and expects everyone else to as well. People who work for a DI can rarely count their time their own. I have known DIs who consider everyone to be on call twenty-four hours a day, seven days a week, fifty-two weeks a year. Because he creates such crises, he must have a staff on which he can depend to get him out of hot water. Partly because of this crisis atmosphere, look for high employee turnover. Unless the rewards outweigh the strain of working for such a disorganized boss, the DI's department will have a swinging door.

There are three more common symptoms of the disorganized incompetent. First, they tend to lose things. Reports, contracts, papers, etc. When confronted, they seldom admit to having received the document in the first place. "Besides," they will say, "just make me another copy, I'm late for a meeting."

Second, to preserve the mask that disorganization creates

for incompetent bosses, they frequently employ "selective memory" (memory they can turn on and off to suit their needs). Recent discussions in which you foretold the folly of continuing to do it the boss's way are magically erased and "never occurred." Usually the result of this discussion places the blame on you.

Finally, the DI boss usually does not have the time to:

(*a*) listen to your oral report on a task he assigned you;

(*b*) read the report on a task he gave you;

(*c*) listen to your oral report summarizing the written report he could not find the time to read.

When this happens, he cannot make an informed decision. To buy some time, the DI will ask some off-the-wall question and conclude that a decision hinges on the answer to his new insightful query, so you had better go back to do some more research.

What to Do

Do not make the common error of overorganizing yourself to compensate for the boss's lacking. This needlessly detracts from your performance. Furthermore, the DI boss may resent it. There are, however, several steps you can take to minimize the DI's intrusion on your workday due to his or her shortcomings.

Instead of preparing detailed written reports that will probably never be read, give him just a brief summary of the key information he needs. Details should stay with you until requested.

Take control of your work load. Do not wait to take charge until a crisis explodes. Begin work well enough in advance to avoid the emergency. If you work in a group, the group can probably manage itself better than the DI boss. Get the group going in that direction. Remember, the less reliance placed on the boss, the less negative effect his disorganization and incompetence will have on you.

Ultimately, you will have to fire the DI boss. He or she will not likely be promoted, and your skills don't develop much from fighting his fires.

Here are the ways to identify a disorganized incompetent, some hazards to watch out for, and different approaches to gain control:

DISORGANIZED INCOMPETENT	
Identifying Characteristics	*Hazards to Watch For*
1. Always late	1. Makes you inefficient and ineffective (can also make you crazy)
2. Never has enough time; poor time manager	2. His/her reputation rubs off on you.
3. Management by crisis; poor planner	3. Little growth potential
4. Misses deadlines	4. High stress environment
5. Shoots from the hip	5. You must work the same unnecessarily long hours.
6. Bad relationships with peers and superiors	
7. Works unnecessarily long hours	

8. Uses selective memory in arguments
9. Poor communicator and an even worse teacher

Approach to Gain Control

1. Don't try to compensate for his/her failings by becoming superorganized.
2. Provide concise summaries of issues and resolutions. Keep details to yourself until requested.
3. Anticipate problems and fix them before they become a source of embarrassment for you.
4. Budget your time. Take over the boss's time budgeting.
5. Fire this boss ASAP!

THE JUVENILE BOSS

The juvenile boss: immature, impatient, egotistical, insecure. Younger than the pleaser boss, the juvenile pictures himself or herself as a prodigy, a superstar, a young Turk. Immature bosses are generally promoted too early by a higher-up who had little concept of basic management skills. *The Peter Principle,* published first in 1969 by the late (and beloved neighbor) Laurence Peter and Raymond Hull, pushes the idea that people are promoted to their level of incompetence. Peter and Hull go on to say that nothing fails (managerially) like success. This holds particularly true for the juvenile boss. Such bosses may have been technically proficient as workers, but they usually lack the experience and depth that make leaders.

Most juvenile bosses attempt to rule with an iron fist. Ego demands that their ideas and leadership abilities are superior exclusively because they are the boss and you are not. Surprisingly, when we bulldoze the accolades associated with fast-track advancement, when we strip away the corporate hierarchy necessary to feed the juvenile boss's ego, we are left with someone possessing a poor self-image. Psychologists trace this overachievement compulsion to a fear of failing.

Whatever the cause, the juvenile boss spells trouble for your career and peace of mind.

Identify the Juvenile Boss

Look closely at the background of suspected juvenile bosses. They were probably considered star performers as workers and possessed some special talent or skill that got them noticed by their bosses. Based on these qualities they were relieved of the task that they did best and promoted to a job for which they were ill prepared. The duties for which a juvenile boss lacks skill are the very tasks needed to be an effective boss. Among these are effective communication, self-confidence, and leadership.

Juvenile bosses are frequently impatient with workers who are not as skilled in their own area of expertise. They show a tendency to grab work from subordinates because "it would take longer to teach you than to just do it myself." Yet bosses are supposed to teach and develop their subordinates.

Observe how juvenile bosses protect their egos. They hide behind the perceived status and superiority that the title of boss allegedly bestows. On the exterior, their projected image attempts to be one of superconfidence and competence—only on the exterior, however. When you get to know the juvenile boss you will find someone afraid of assaults on his authority, someone who thinks he should have all the answers and fears admitting when he does not. The tougher things get for the juvenile boss, the more he will dig in his heels, insisting on the merits of his approach.

Have you ever seen a boss backed into a corner where all logic said that he was wrong only to have the discussion abruptly dismissed with a wave of the boss's hand and him making a "command decision"? If so, you were probably looking at a juvenile boss.

Some envy the outward appearance of the juvenile boss. So young, so bright, so upwardly mobile. Their insecurity, however, can be detrimental to subordinates. Work done by anyone other than the boss rarely measures up. Acceptable work (a rare thing indeed to the juvenile boss) always seems to use an approach that contains some fault. The juvenile boss wields the sting of excessive criticism like a master swordsman. The backhanded compliment, unleashed with devastating accuracy, becomes his put-away shot. It would not do to have someone of equal ability right under his nose to compete for the title of wunderkind.

What to Do

The juvenile boss has several traits that, if properly harnessed, can be put to good use. The juvenile boss enjoys the confidence of management. He acquired the reputation of being bright, energetic, and on the way up. A certain amount of his image of success rubs off on you just by association. People assume that subordinates contribute to at least some of the superstar's success. Though probably lacking in training ability, the juvenile boss can probably teach you something about your job.

The approach to firing the juvenile boss should retain the good aspects of being close to him or her. Don't try to prove yourself better than he is or attempt to transfer from his department. Instead, reduce the amount of direct supervision he exerts. Seize control over your work. Make sure that the projects you work on are personally important to the juvenile boss. This will keep him involved in your career so that:

- You can learn what makes him so good;
- He will be less likely to disagree with your approach and conclusions because he was intimately involved;
- You are more likely to be one of the key success factors for the project;
- A bonding will occur, allowing you to be caught up in his whirlwind so that you ascend along with your boss;
- You may become a valued and trusted subordinate. Your value comes from knowing how your juvenile boss thinks and the most effective method of presentation to communicate both your thoughts.

With close involvement in your work, the juvenile boss is less likely to criticize you. Less likely, but not out of the question. If deserved, such criticism should be accepted with grace. Be sure to learn from the incident and never repeat the error. If unfairly leveled, say so forcefully while keeping the juvenile boss's ego out of it. With the juvenile boss you can never win an argument that involves a question of his authority or competence. These are his lifelines. He will defend them to the death—yours, if you're not careful.

Here are the ways to identify a juvenile boss, some hazards to watch out for, and different approaches to gain control:

JUVENILE BOSS

Identifying Characteristics

1. Egotistical, young, bright, upwardly mobile

2. Was a proficient worker; not an effective leader

3. Tends to be domineering

4. Has a poor self-image

5. Not a good communicator or teacher

6. Prone to do the job himself

7. Ends discussions when backed into a corner

Hazards to Watch For

1. Unless you effectively manage him, you won't learn a thing.

2. Will always place you in his/her shadow

3. Will grab credit for your work

4. Your ego will be deflated by this boss.

Approach to Gain Control

1. Get close to the boss.
2. Learn how he thinks. Understand what his standards are.
3. Become an integral part of his/her success formula.
4. Learn what made him/her a star.
5. Ask for help when you need it.
6. Accept criticism when warranted, and learn from it.

> 7. Never challenge his/her authority
>   or competence—these are his/her
>   lifelines.

THE LOCOMOTIVE BOSS

Justly named, the locomotive boss will roll right over your career unless derailed. If your personality requires the milk of human kindness, you'd better look for another cow. He relies on brute force rather than finesse to get the job of management done. Like the juvenile boss, the locomotive has little tolerance for any challenge to his authority.

The locomotive boss has a huge psychological investment in his career. When faced with new subordinates who may have a state-of-the-art degree in a discipline closely related to the job, his psyche demands that he defend his superiority. He probably came up through the ranks with little formal training in his particular specialty. He believes that there is no substitute for OJT (on-the-job training).

The locomotive boss can dish out more heartache than any other boss category. As a race, they are rude, indifferent to subordinates' feelings, and are frequently stuck in dead-end jobs themselves. Having failed to prove their worth to their own bosses, they must try to prove it to their subordinates.

With more and more women moving up the corporate ladder, you should not be surprised to learn that some of them fall into the previously exclusive male bastion of the locomotive boss. If you think that women can't bully, browbeat, or terrorize their people, you're in for a rude awakening. In the business world, underestimating the animal tenacity of a female locomotive can be lethal to your career. In 1989 *California* magazine ran an article on the worst bosses. Several women made this august list. Two such "stellar performers" were appropriately termed "hell on heels" and "the queen of mean."

Did You Get the Number of that Locomotive?

You don't have to see the locomotive boss to know he's there—just listen. Locomotives tend to shout and scream at their subordinates. Somehow they assume that the rest of us are hard of hearing. Further, the locomotive boss always knows everything about the subject under discussion. Ego demands that the locomotive never be wrong, especially in front of an audience.

Watch how the locomotive delegates authority—didn't see much, did you? Because her arrogance assumes that nobody can do the job as well as she, the locomotive has a hard time delegating anything. On those rare occasions when authority does get delegated, watch the locomotive oversupervise to the point where he may as well have done it himself. Does your boss take a vacation, then call the office fighting fires (creating some, too) and staying involved so often that she may as well have never left? If so, you may have a locomotive for a boss.

Locomotives allow too many subordinates to report directly to them. They do this to preserve both their responsibility and authority. This habit may have developed as a temporary solution to help new employees who were unfamiliar with their jobs. Soon the locomotive becomes the bottleneck by insisting that everything flow through him. Consequently, he spreads himself too thin, always running from fire to fire like a pyromaniac.

Take an honest appraisal of the people a suspect locomotive has working for him (yourself included). Generally the personality types of a locomotive's subordinates are weaker than the boss's. The locomotive's ego can't stand competition. Does your department have an unhappy history of losing the brightest, most talented people? When asked why they are leaving, do the responses involve a need for more responsibility, additional authority, and fresh growth potential? If so, the engine driving the train has run over these people.

Locomotives have a hard time teaching, trusting, and communicating. After receiving instructions from your boss, do you honestly believe that you understand the task, only to be accused later of not having listened to instructions? If so, the problem may not be yours.

Observe the way your locomotive boss motivates his or her subordinates. Usually, stimulus comes from fear of the boss throwing a tantrum or of later reprisal. People do not do something for a locomotive boss out of affection for the person. Have you ever heard someone who works for a locomotive say that they like the guy and want to do everything possible to help him out? Of course not, because he doesn't deserve such loyalty.

Watch the locomotive sabotage an unwary subordinate. He will knowingly let out just enough rope for you to hang yourself, then gleefully watch you swing in the breeze.

What to Do

Most of us are naturally inclined to stay away from the locomotive. Of course, it would be easier to hide from him. Resist this tendency. Sooner or later, you'll be caught in a tunnel with nothing but the locomotive's headlight barreling straight toward you.

Instead, move toward the locomotive. Make the locomotive's concerns your concerns. Stay so involved that you've already handled minor problems before they explode and cause yet another tirade. When confronted by the locomotive (probably in a screaming fit), stand your ground. If you know that you are right, say so. Do not argue with the locomotive, and be sure to allow him or her to save face. Derail the runaway engine by agreeing with her. This takes most of the wind out of her sails. How can you argue with someone who agrees with everything you say?

Have you heard the locomotive boss ask, "Am I the only one around here who understands the problem?" This represents the starting line for him. Stop the locomotive cold by making him realize that you do indeed understand the problem and share his concern. Your response should be forceful and convincing, never patronizing or sarcastic. From this point you have punctured at least half of the issue (nobody understands but me . . .). You can both work on a solution to the problem and leave behind the reasons it occurred in the first place. Locomotives want to assign blame (always on someone else). Steer the discussion away from this unproductive territory. Except when a subordinate deliberately tries to sabotage the locomotive (not uncommon), placing blame doesn't get anyone anywhere.

Never get into a verbal shoving match. You'll always lose. Don't try to defend your actions by insisting that the locomotive knew about the problem or actually assisted in creating the problem (even if he did). You want to win the entire war, not just a minor battle.

Here are the ways to identify a locomotive boss, some hazards to watch out for, and different approaches to gain control:

LOCOMOTIVE BOSS

Identifying Characteristics	*Hazards to Watch For*
1. Uses brute force to manage subordinates	1. Emotionally trying to work for this type of boss
2. Shouts and throws temper tantrums at subordinates	2. Job problems caused by boss can create domestic problems.
3. Defends his authority to the death	3. Low probability of advancement
4. Huge psychological investment in his/her career; often the career is his/her only source of positive recognition.	4. Critical of subordinates not only to their faces, but to others in the company
5. Well seasoned; probably came up through the ranks	
6. Insensitive to subordinates' feelings or career needs	
7. Little upward mobility for the boss	
8. Can't delegate authority	

9. Uses an overbearing, authoritarian approach to management

Approach to Gain Control
1. Get close to the locomotive.
2. Gain the locomotive's confidence.
3. Solve problems before they explode into major issues.
4. When confronted, stand your ground. Authority respects strong people, especially when you are right.
5. Don't accuse the locomotive of being wrong—you'll always lose.

Now that you have a good idea of your type of boss, you know how to identify him or her, and generally you understand what to do about the problem, you are ready for the next step: Ax your boss and become your own supervisor. This will cure some of the most obvious symptoms of a problem boss.

II

Ax Your Boss: Becoming Your Own Supervisor

To her dismay, Alice discovered herself in a classic dilemma. Day after frustrating day she confronted a belligerent boss who insisted on oversupervising. Her low self-esteem showed up in every action. Her boss placed as little confidence in her as she did . . . until she fired him and became her own supervisor.

Alice's metamorphosis began with a frank discussion and some self-asserting talk. Gradually, Alice divorced herself from the daily grind of having her boss make all the decisions. Soon Alice seized more responsibility and depended less on her boss for approval. New confidence in her skills became apparent, even to her boss. Alice fully grasped her liberation when her boss admitted that such close supervision needlessly dribbled away his time. When her boss offered, she jumped at the promotion to lead person in her group and the added supervisory responsibility.

Weak bosses who never made the transition from worker to manager will smother their subordinates with oversupervision if given the opportunity. Further, bosses who prove to be incompetent managers likely developed from incompetent workers. You do not need such a person showing you how to do your job. If allowed to continue they will harm your performance and, eventually, your career. They must be fired as your boss.

FORCE YOUR BOSS TO DO HIS JOB, NOT YOURS

Three types of bosses tend to oversupervise if allowed: Imagonna Grabontoitz, the disorganized incompetent; I. B. Meantuu, the locomotive; and Lame Duk, the politician. Each, however, oversupervises for different reasons. Poor communication skills and self-inflicted time pressures cause the disorganized incompetent to oversupervise just to get the results she wants when she wants them. Locomotives like I. B. Meantuu have a difficult time delegating anything. As a result they tend to do much of the work themselves. Management theorists call this hyperresponsibility reverse delegation. Furthermore, the locomotive needlessly cracks the whip in order to retain his authority and superiority over subordinates. Lame Duk, the politician, demonstrates his paranoia about someone forming an adverse political liaison by insisting that he be informed (and approve) of every minute detail of every task, not only in his department but (preferably) everywhere else as well.

If allowed to continue, such oversupervision will perpetuate your unnecessary dependency on an undeserving boss. With dependency comes a lack of control over your career. A true manager does not get paid to do the job of his subordinates. Management means that the boss supervises to ensure proper direction and control. Bosses who try not only to manage but to do the task as well will ultimately fail at both. The result will be an overworked, overstressed supervisor whose shop produces sloppy work.

When the boss trusts you and has confidence in your work, she will be less inclined to oversupervise. When she no longer feels the need to smother the staff with oversupervision, she can begin to do her real job: managing, planning, and advising. This makes for a happier workplace, more autonomy for subordinates, professional growth, confidence to exercise independent judgment, and higher quality production.

There are ways to force your boss to do his job, not yours. When he sees your ability to operate independently, even the thickest boss will slack off. A new respect for your abilities replaces the distrust such boss types have for their subordinates.

REMOVE UNNECESSARY SUPERVISION

Bosses, especially the juvenile and locomotive, feel that the staff requires their direct and constant supervision to get the job done right. Yet, today's enlightened business environment has falsified this more than ever before. It used to be that only the boss saw the big picture. Therefore, only he or she could integrate the department's work product into that of the rest of the company. Today, with more participative management techniques and subordinates whose diverse backgrounds allow for more familiarity with many facets of the operation, this notion has become archaic. Certainly it has no place in your supervision requirements.

Unneeded supervision gets in the way of your work. Many inept bosses hang over their subordinates' shoulders without contributing much to the work product. The juvenile boss wants to know everything that goes on to the point of "micro managing" your work. The locomotive boss wants to feel needed and will become an albatross around your neck if permitted. Further, he lies in wait to catch you doing something wrong, then pounces. Achieve self-supervision so that the boss can't smother you.

BECOME SELF-SUPERVISING

Getting the boss off your back requires you to earn her trust. Confidence in your work product, your ability to manage your time, and knowing that you will ask questions when necessary goes a long way toward gaining your boss's respect. When your boss sees that her intervention detracts from the work being done, even the simplest bosses will go away. Let's discuss the steps needed to become self-supervising.

TIME MANAGEMENT

Your time should top the list of priceless commodities. Don't waste it. Some bosses believe that employees will dribble away company time unless ridden hard. It's up to you to demonstrate that this may be true of others, but not of you.

Start each day by making a list of the things you will accomplish that day. This may sound rudimentary, but things put in writing tend to become cast in stone. If you stick to your list each day you will have accomplished something. Soon you will begin selecting your daily lists with particular strategies in mind. Strategies designed to fire your boss and keep her fired.

Identify those people who waste your time. Stay away from them. Some bored employees aimlessly walk the halls. They'll come into your workplace and flop down in a chair, get comfy, and proceed to tell you how overworked they are. Say in plain English that you're busy and could the two of you talk at lunch or meet for a drink after work. If that doesn't help, stand up. There exists an irresistible force in nature to stand when your host stands. Then simply guide the intruder out of your space and get back to work.

Plan how to deal with interruptions. Most people in business get interrupted. Dealing with emergencies that must be handled immediately are part of the job. It takes practice, however, to distinguish between a true emergency and a "routine" interruption. I have studied interruptions; most have four parts:

- A beginning where the interrupter socializes with banter irrelevant to the problem.
- A statement as to the purpose of the interruption.
- Agreement on the course of action.
- An ending where the interrupter again socializes with banter irrelevant to the problem.

You can cut through much of this by controlling the interruption. Here's how: First, do not stop work or break your train of thought just because someone comes into your space and begins talking. Finish your thought or wait until you come to a good stopping point before giving the interloper your attention. You may want to write yourself a quick note of where you left off. Second, before the person gets rolling on her social banter, ask the reason for her interruption. Third, with your complete attention on the interrupter, solve the problem, delegate, or give direction as required. Finally, while you still have the floor, boot her out with some nicety such as, "I'm glad that one is solved. Now I can get back to my project which is due in two hours." Even the most obtuse individual will get the message.

If your work space has a door, close it if necessary to keep the rabble out. This includes the boss who drops by to shoot the breeze. The pleaser thinks you need his pep talk. The juvenile and locomotive think that you can't get along without their input. The politician wants to see if you've any information she can use. The disorganized incompetent forgot why he dropped by in the first place. Whatever their reasons, keep the conversation short, dispose of them as quickly as possible, and get back to work.

This can be more difficult if you find yourself in the no-man's-land of the boss's own office. There, you have less control over the space and the interruption. I once observed a disorganized incompetent with the attention span of a four-year-old (about thirty seconds). Just when his subordinates thought they had his complete concentration, someone would walk by his office, his head would come up, eyes would unglaze for a moment, and he would call out, "John, have you got a second?" Concentration abruptly ended, and he would fritter away his subordinates' time. So devoid of any courtesy was this same individual, that he had a private "hot" phone line installed. His three- and four-year-old children had but to lift the receiver at home to talk with Daddy. The boss's phone would ring incessantly, and again he would dribble away his subordinates' time.

Control your time in the boss's office as much as possible. Schedule definite beginnings and endings bounded by, say, another appointment afterward. Under a time constraint, the boss may be more likely to stick to the point. Don't be afraid to close the door to the boss's office to avoid interruptions from the hall monitors. Make a deal with the boss's secretary not to interrupt with phone calls unless they are urgent.

Where possible, establish the outcome of decisions to be made at group meetings before the meeting starts. This does two things: First, it saves everyone valuable time by making them think through their arguments and positions in advance. Second, if you need a particular decision made, it allows you time to do some lobbying on your own behalf.

Cut short useless telephone calls. Just as people walk the halls searching for company, some use the phone for the same purpose. Resist the urge to chat about things that don't help you get your job done. I've had associates call my Los Angeles office from New York, hastily complete the business portion of the call, then want to discuss the weather. My response is always the same: "It's a beautiful day. My office overlooks the harbor, and I'm sitting here watching a sailboat go by, thinking how much work I have to get done." This has the same effect as standing up and bouncing the uninvited and disruptive guest.

Don't be guilty of using the phone to validate your own importance as the locomotive boss tends to do. Your calls should be brief, for a definite purpose and accomplish what you wanted, period. After all, both your boss and subordinates may have read this book, too. We don't want you to be the kind of person who "the folks" want to fire.

Keep a calendar. This helps to block out periods where you need to accomplish particular tasks as well as avoid embarrassing scheduling conflicts (suffered by the disorganized incompetent). One person I know who successfully became a self-supervisor blocked out what she called slop periods at the end of each day. Such periods were designed to be free time to catch up on things that didn't get done but should have. She carefully protected her slop periods from interruptions. She didn't panic if a task scheduled for completion somehow got waylaid. It would be done during the slop period at the end of the day. On the last Friday of the month, if her slop periods were not used up, she would reward herself by leaving the office early with a clear conscience.

If you have a secretary or assistant, ask them to screen your calls and your visitors. This may appear that you are simply flexing your corporate muscles. On the contrary, a good secretary can save hours of otherwise wasted time for you.

WORK EFFECTIVELY

Working effectively means that you do the right things to get the job done. Avoid wandering down paths that, though interesting, do not get you to the desired end result. Bosses who oversupervise do so in part because they want their employees to work effectively (a laudable objective). They just don't know when to stop.

To ensure that you do the right things to get a specific result, stop and think about the job. Plan the task step by step. Do things in the order that will produce the desired outcome in the least amount of time. If someone has taught you to do the job and part of the task being taught doesn't make sense, chances are it's wrong. Stop and question the teacher. If it still doesn't make sense, get another teacher.

Often in corporate folklore, tasks are handed down from one generation to the next without questioning the reasons for certain things or revising procedures. This can needlessly add to your task without improving the result. Question authority. Be certain of an accurate information source. I heard a story in which a child asked her mother why she always would cut the end off of the roast before putting it in the pan to bake. She said that was the way grandmother had taught her to cook a roast. When grandmother was asked why she cut off the end of the roast, she said this was the way great-grandmother had taught her to cook a roast. When great-grandmother was asked why she cut off the end of the roast, she said it was because she never had a big enough pan! Question authority.

WORK EFFICIENTLY

Simply put, the efficient person does things right the first time. Time spent redoing a task is time wasted.

Further, you will (deservedly so) catch your boss's attention by producing shabby work that needs to be corrected. The disorganized incompetent puts such time pressure on her subordinates that those who do not produce accurate work the first time are seldom around to do it again. Similarly, the locomotive looks for inefficiencies in his people, then attacks. This confirms his mistaken notion that the folks need him.

The disorganized incompetent uses accuracy as an excuse. He will say that the project was late (a usual occurrence) because it needed to be accurate. Who can fault someone for wanting to be right? We can, however, blame him for swallowing an unreasonable deadline in the first place. He should have known the complexities of the task and how long it would take to get it right. We can denounce him for procrastination in organizing the job and delegating assignments. We can blame him for being such a poor communicator that no one can understand his instructions. Finally, we can condemn him for having such poor relations with his peers in other departments that outside help is out of the question.

Efficient workers segment an assignment into its component parts and assign priorities to each. They have both timing and quality goals for each part of the job. They watch and guide each element of the task so that it turns out as specified when needed. Efficient workers are much easier to trust. With trust comes the gift of autonomy and independence. The boss knows you will do those things necessary to get the job done (effectiveness) and that the final product will be right (efficiency).

SELF-RELIANCE

Freedom from stifling oversupervision goes to those who demonstrate the ability to work independently.

Problems that appear mind-boggling to others are anticipated and overcome routinely by self-reliance. To break the
noose that an overbearing boss has around your neck,
demonstrate an ability to solve problems yourself. Rather
than run to your boss at the slightest problem (the locomotives just love this), try solving it yourself. If necessary seek
advice from co-workers or from other departments. If you
must go to the boss for help, present the issue like this:

- State the problem;
- Identify the desired result;
- Describe what solutions you've already explored and
  why they weren't acceptable;
- Identify alternative solutions that have potential but
  weren't tried and why;
- Ask for your boss's opinion as to what you should do
  next.

When couched like this, you are treating the boss with
respect, as a peer, and flattering her by asking her opinion
(both the juvenile and the locomotive enjoy this part). You
are not asking her to do your job for you, nor do you want
that. Furthermore, you have demonstrated a high degree of
independence by exploring solutions on your own before
asking for help.

Do not act in a vacuum. This can be fatal especially when
dealing with Lyan Lobby, the political boss. Be sure to ask
for his input early. Doubtless he will see monumental
political obstacles that passed over your head. No matter.
There exists the remote possibility that your boss may be of
some help, so you must keep him informed of what you are
doing. Furthermore, asking for help puts you in control of
the supervision being requested. Subordinates who regulate
the "help" given by their bosses limit the destructive
interference an uncontrolled boss can inflict. Finally, by
asking questions and not working in a vacuum, you are

more likely to hit the target your boss (and his boss) had in mind on the first try.

Your boss can be a source of information, but she's not the only one nor is she necessarily the best. Hire secret help. Use friends, spouses, paid outside experts. Read the latest trade journals. Join industry trade groups. Talk with your counterparts at other firms. There are multitudes of sources for new ideas. No one has to know where you got them.

My wife, a securities broker, called me late one afternoon and said that she needed my undivided attention that night—hurrah! We worked until midnight drafting a proposal for her firm's largest client. The client liked the proposal and brought her product. The day belonged to my wife. Do you think she said, "Thanks, guys, but the credit should really go to Chris?"

The autonomy that comes from relying on your own knowledge, resources, and skills can be both scary and exhilarating. After a while, you'll find that your own abilities can take you farther than you thought. Those who truly believe in their own skills (and usually have the right answers) are acknowledged by the rest of the staff as informal leaders. The unnecessary supervision exercised over them by substandard bosses becomes minimal. These are the people who succeeded in taking charge of their careers and firing their bosses.

Don't always trust the so-called experts. They often don't know any more than you do. The "all-knowing" directors of IBM could have bought fledgling Haloid Corp. for a minimal investment. They didn't want to take the risk and they saw no future in the product. Haloid eventually changed its name to what it is today—Xerox. I once interviewed the editor of a leading computer magazine. He confessed that a kid from northern California once showed him a tiny computer and asked for his marketing help in exchange for equity in his and his friend's new company.

The editor refused, stating he didn't have the time. This disappointed Steve Jobs greatly but not so much that it deterred him from starting Apple Computer. If you want further proof as to the faith you should place in yourself over that which you place in your boss, consider what blunders your boss has made lately.

Don't be afraid to make a decision and live with it. Many subordinates like to complain about their boss being over-bearing. Yet when faced with taking responsibility for a decision and living with it, they become weak-kneed. Few business decisions have a clear answer. If they did, we would not need bosses. Usually you will have to wait (often until it's too late) to find out how correct you were. Nevertheless, taking responsibility and making decisions will gain you freedom from an incompetent boss.

This works especially well for disorganized incompetents and politicians. The DI can't make decisions and will look for someone on whom he can lean. The politician who can trust a subordinate to be her deputy will have that much more time to schmooze.

POSITION YOUR BOSS AS AN ADVISER

Becoming your own supervisor requires you to think of your boss as your peer, not your master. If you believe it, soon the boss will come around as well. Like a snowball rolling faster and faster downhill, the greater responsibility you seize, the more independent decisions you will make and the more of a leader you will become. As your role takes shape, the easier it will be for the boss to accept you as a peer and provide advice rather than stifling oversupervision. With your boss less involved in the minutia of your job, the less your career depends on him.

As your leadership capacity grows, so too does the boss's respect for your professional abilities. It naturally follows that she will begin to think of herself less as your master and more as a director and adviser if she can rely on you to get the job done on time, as specified without her help.

We want your boss to respect you as a person, as your own supervisor, and as professionally competent. People who are wishy-washy find it tougher to gain such respect. To amass an image of professional competence, think through each communication with your boss beforehand. Let the boss know you've done your homework on a topic by having statistics on the tip of your tongue that support your conclusions and uphold your decisions. Try to anticipate your boss's objections, questions, fears, and hidden motivations about a proposal you may be making. Address these issues as part of your presentation. This way, you maintain the upper hand and control the discussion. The locomotive boss, when subjected to such unexpected competence, finds it more difficult to gather steam and roll over you.

Look at the results of a proposal made by someone who "promises the idea will work" or who "guarantees X amount of sales as the result." Bosses can't respect mere promises, nor can they take such fluff to their own boss and sell it. Don't make a proposal filled with personal guarantees and platitudes. Instead, try making your proposal along these lines:

- Here's the plan, and here's *why* I think it will work.
- The plan is expected to increase sales by X number of dollars, and here is how I arrived at that number.
- This is how much the plan will cost item by item.
- I will personally monitor progress. Here are my intermediate goals.
- If in 90 days I haven't met XYZ goals, we scuttle the strategy and cut our losses. Losses at that point are expected to be X dollars, and here is how I arrived at that number.

- Here is my contingency plan in case we have to bail out.
- I've positioned the staff to begin next Monday.

This type of presentation demonstrates several things about you: It proclaims that you have the courage of your convictions, the open-mindedness to address the possibility that you may be wrong and have taken steps to protect the company from such an unlikely occurrence. Additionally, it points out that you understand the relationship between risk and reward and have quantified both. It shows that you have the presence of mind to plan ahead. This method backs up assertions with facts and figures. There is little wishful thinking here, and the presentation does not come across like mush. Finally, you have left little doubt that the boss will concur by including an assumptive close.

A presentation containing the steps shown above gives the boss something concrete to sell. Your boss will probably have to take you along to her boss to sell the plan. Obviously you know far more about the subject than she could hope to in the time allotted. A presentation with such an outcome signals a significant decline in your immediate boss's influence over your career. This enhances your professional reputation both within your department and to the rest of your company. Further, you have placed the boss's boss in a position to personally judge the merits of your work. Now your future rests less in the hands of someone whom you found it necessary to fire from your career.

Workaholic bosses measure people's abilities by their own twisted standard: number of hours worked. To them, you can never be a peer until you demonstrate the same perverted dedication to the job as they do. Overcome this problem by making the boss measure your contribution by results, not by hours worked.

Imagonna Grabontoitz, like most disorganized incompetents, is a workaholic. To make the transition from peon to peer with this type of boss you need to demonstrate that you can make your deadlines and exceed (not just meet) quality requirements without excessive overtime. Additionally, let the boss know that you have a life apart from the office. Tell her about your family or vacation plans. Rather than dissuade you from living the rest of your life, the boss (unless she's totally incorrigible) will likely be envious of your ability to work effectively and efficiently while pursuing other interests.

Most of the unusually successful people I know have created a healthy balance between work and play. Of course they work long hours; usually ten to twelve hours a day. But that doesn't necessarily make them workaholics. What they do with the remainder of the day when they are not working makes the difference. These thriving people have learned to leave the office behind them. They have enough self-confidence to know how good they are and enough self-respect to reward themselves with playtime once the job is completed. In fact, playtime becomes the most fertile area for unconsciously rejuvenating their creativity for their jobs.

As long as your boss knows that you are indeed committed, reliable, and do excellent work, you'll have little trouble being accepted as a peer even by the workaholic boss.

The boss's weaknesses should become your strengths. This will not only create dependence on you, but will also gain respect from the boss. Complementary skills don't have to be anything extraordinary. For example, if your boss happens to be a poor writer, take over most of her duties in this area. If you need to, take a writing class to brush up on this necessary skill. If your boss shares a fear of computers, become the computer expert yourself. With the innovations you'll be able to implement, your stock will rise to the top of the charts in no time.

One final point about becoming a peer rather than remaining just another of the folks: become interested in the boss as a person. The saying "It's lonely at the top" carries a grain of truth (so does "Misery loves company"). Bosses often feel that no one understands the strain they are under. Miserable bosses will try to make you that way, too. Get to know the boss. Show him that you are interested. Find out what excites the boss and what he does not like. Empathize with your boss. In other words, look at the situation from his point of view. Be aware of your boss's political friends and enemies. Understand that the pleaser may have a shrew for a wife and gets respect only at the office. Recognize the hazards to which the disorganized incompetent appears oblivious. Find out what the juvenile boss did to become a superstar, and duplicate the parts you like.

QUALITY CONTROL

There are few nobler objectives than to ax your maladroit boss and become your own supervisor. Once done, however, you must deliver. Your production should incorporate your own fresh ideas. Likewise, it must be what the boss needs, not just what she said she wanted. Often a difference exists, and it's up to you to be aware of it.

When you receive an assignment, resist the urge to jump right in with both feet and start working. The disorganized incompetent makes this particularly tempting because you receive most of your assignments from him with an unreasonable deadline. Remain calm. Instead of jumping off the ledge, step back and find out what caused the need for the assignment in the first place. Next, ask how your work will be used when completed. Find out who will be the audience for your work if you are preparing a study, report, or will be delivering a speech.

If you are given directions by your boss, determine if those directions make sense and if they will produce the required result. Look carefully at the deadline. Better to let the boss know about any problems on the front end while time exists to fix it than after it's too late. Ascertain how much detail the assignment really requires. You can always get more detailed if needed, but you can never regain time wasted on excesses that do not enhance the work product.

Develop an approach to completing the assignment. If necessary, create a plan designating what steps need to be done. Formulate a clear picture of what the finished work product will be. If this differs from the way the boss described it originally, talk with her about it. Make sure she understands exactly what you intend to produce and when. This again reinforces your independence and ability to think on your own. Let her know of your progress periodically. Doing this allows you to control the level of supervision you get.

Determine before you start how precise you must be. Your level of precision will dictate how often your work gets tested (by you, or preferably, by someone else). Make sure that you stay within your predetermined tolerance for error. If you find mistakes, either fix your procedures or increase your review.

Quality control does not ensure that you produce perfect work. After all, we're only human. It does mean, however, that any errors are recognized and accepted as being within our tolerance for error. Simply put, perfection is both expensive and usually unnecessary. You would be surprised to learn that when the locomotive roars that a job must be perfect, he often means that within ninety to ninety-five percent is OK.

When you formulate your approach to an assignment,

install checkpoints along the way so that you can monitor accuracy. For example, if you are supposed to keep the corporate bank account straight, why wait until the end of the month to reconcile the account? If you have a problem bank account, try doing the reconciliation once a week or even every day if necessary. If you type lots of memos and letters but are a poor speller, get word-processing software that has an electronic spell checker, dictionary, and thesaurus.

If your job requires you to perform a number of voluminous, repetitive procedures, try testing small samples of the job to draw a conclusion on the accuracy of the entire task as it progresses. The captain of a ship delegates steering to others. But he does periodically check position against his planned course. This allows for mid-course corrections without much lost time.

Part of auditing progress includes checking problem indicators from other departments. To control the quality of your work, you must become sensitive to danger signals from the rest of the company. For example, failure to collect receivables will result in complaints from the cash manager at having to borrow more money.

Accuracy and acceptable quality are two things that will allow you to regain your freedom from an inept boss. Bosses who oversupervise do so, in part, from fear that the subordinate will make mistakes without help. In truth, quality work products are usually produced in spite of help from the boss. Your history of successfully completing assignments without help from the boss will put you well on the road to gaining your independence.

TOOLS FOR AXING YOUR BOSS

There are nine key tools used to ax your boss and become your own supervisor:

1. Force the boss to do his or her job, not yours;
2. Eliminate unnecessary supervision;
3. Become self-supervising;
4. Manage your own time rather than relying on your boss to do it for you;
5. Work effectively;
6. Work efficiently;
7. Practice self-reliance;
8. Position your boss as a peer and adviser;
9. Control your own work quality.

People who diligently practice and employ these methods have little trouble reducing the negative impact of most types of bosses. Few actions speak louder about your ability to manage your work by yourself than consistently producing a quality product on time without assistance from your boss. Given time, even the most obtuse bosses will get the message.

Once you've become your own supervisor, you are well on the road to firing your boss. We're not done yet, however, not by any means. Next we want to dominate the boss in all aspects of the job. You know you've succeeded when the boss starts coming to you for advice.

III

Dominate Your Boss: Making Them Thank You for It

I gave Maggie, a Scottish terrier puppy, to my wife as a gift. We enjoyed puppydom for about an hour. Then Maggie, not having been taught any better, lost her bladder on the carpet (*Author's note:* A product called Nature's Miracle, found in most pet shops, works wonders). Swift and immediate training began with a folded newspaper, then a scolding, and finally, a hasty pitch out the dog door. This went on for several days until we realized that we had taught Maggie the wrong thing. She still went on the carpet, then ran for her life out the dog door. I quickly changed the routine from negative to positive reinforcement. Instead of waiting for the offense to occur, then striking, we anticipated the need. Maggie was invited outside, then when the proper behavior occurred we enthusiastically congratulated her. This most basic rule established us as the boss. With control now firmly grounded, it became easy to expand Maggie's repertoire of behaviors using the same positive-teaching techniques.

How quickly the failings of an incompetent boss can become our own. Failure has a tendency to become shared with (or better yet, blamed on) subordinates while the actual circumstances that finger the true culprit rarely surface. Some bosses who screw up even finish in a better position when they brush off the real cause of the problem and magnanimously accept responsibility because "it happened on their watch." My, what lofty values these bosses must have to protect their people by shouldering the blame themselves. The fact that the subordinates did not need protecting in the first place quickly vanishes. The political boss has evolved as an expert at shifting the blame and twisting failure into a moral victory.

NECESSITY FOR DOMINANCE

Dominance over your boss and job ensures that at least you control your own destiny, not some unfit boob. There are three areas of your relationship with the boss that you must dominate:

- Instructions and methods for doing the job;
- Amount and type of criticism;
- Responsibilities and authority.

Failure at any of these three points gives your boss permission to use you and your career as he would any other floor mat.

Control means that you—not your boss—set the guidelines. Bosses and everyone else respect people who refuse to be trod upon by unaware or insensitive masters. As long as you have a legitimate position and are not viewed as contrary or disagreeable, you can come out on top in these three areas.

If you aspire to take your boss's place, you must not only have his respect but that of his boss as well. When choosing between two people who are equally well qualified as candidates for promotion, the winner will be the person who has earned the most respect among the staff and management. Make sure your boss has no qualms about your ability to handle subordinates or other potentially hostile situations (such as customers) by the way you handled him. I. B. Meantuu, the locomotive boss, has been known to give respected subordinates a backhanded compliment, saying with pride, "I know she can handle the folks, look how she handled me, and I'm one tough SOB!" When we speak of "seasoning," the meaning often translates into one's ability to prevail over a tough adversary. The first such test of seasoning tells how well you have wrestled the responsibilities of supervision, instruction, criticism, and authority away from your boss.

Dominance over your boss means that you call the shots with respect to how you are treated. By controlling the major management issues between you and the boss, you clearly define your responsibilities and the authority you have to get the job done. Such dominance does not have to be a power struggle. When done correctly, it ends with the boss thinking of you as an excellent self-starter.

Dominance over the boss also increases the distance you can place between you and his failures. When you have become the acknowledged master over your job, with little interference from the boss, you become a sovereign island in a stormy sea. The greatest distance occurs when you know more about your job than your boss does. At that point, you are clearly in the driver's seat. If you are lucky, the boss's boss will also acknowledge your independence and begin treating you autonomously. When this happens, the incompetent boss can't lay a glove on you. You no longer have the need for direct supervision from him or for instructions on how to do particular aspects of the job. Any criticism your boss may level at you (the locomotive probably won't quit trying) will have little impact on your career progress. Responsibility for doing your job rests with you, as does access to resources that help get the job done.

There are two particular bosses who must be dominated if at all possible: the pleaser and the locomotive. The pleaser will damage your career by trying to keep everyone happy instead of doing his job. In so doing, he will compromise your work product as well. Pleasers have not learned that management sometimes means making decisions with which not everyone agrees but must tolerate. Results are seen in the mediocre work the pleaser and her group of underlings produce. This will contaminate you if you are not careful. The good news is that the pleaser can be more easily dominated than any other boss type.

Locomotives make life just plain miserable. They are nasty, overbearing, and crack the whip of authority just to hear it snap. Locomotives do get the job done, but their subordinates are burned out afterward. Dominating this type of boss will reduce the stress with which you live. Care must be taken not to allow this phase of firing your boss to degenerate into a struggle for corporate survival. You probably can't completely dominate someone as skilled as the locomotive using only the sheer force of your personality. There are, however, subtle but effective ways that will bring him to heel.

TRAIN THE BOSS TO OBEY

Keep domination of your boss as simple as possible. Like the example of Maggie the Scottie, we must be sure that we send the right signals to the boss. People (as well as pets and children) learn by example. If you want your locomotive boss to stop screaming at you, you could start by not screaming yourself. Additionally, people need signals as to the acceptability of their behavior. The child who gets orally chastised followed by a spanking will soon get the message. Likewise, and much more effective, the child who gets rewarded for doing something will remember and try to duplicate the behavior when he wants the same reward. In a slightly more sophisticated manner, we will use this approach with your boss. Before you do anything, however, the boss must be receptive.

Assertive Listening

Listening cannot be stressed enough. To make sure the boss listens to you, begin by making sure she knows that you are listening to her. Start this process by catching, then retaining eye contact when talking to your boss. People distrust the word of someone who cannot look them in the eye. Further, things that are not important enough to require eye contact could not have been that important to begin with.

Along with eye contact comes your reaction to what the boss says. Take care that your body language sends the right signals. Become an active listener. Nod that you understand what the boss says. Use your facial expression to form some sort of reaction to the conversation. Do not just sit there passively like a bump on a log. Remember, the days of the boss dictating to you are over. If she says something you don't understand, you don't agree with, or you need clarified, jump right in. Practice two-way conversations with your boss. Not only do you get more out of them, but your boss knows that you are interested and that you are unafraid to assert yourself. People who say they had to bite their tongue to keep from saying something are not in a position to dominate their boss.

Ask open-ended questions. Open-ended questions are those that cannot be answered with one word. They are designed to draw the other person's thoughts into the open. Such questions begin with words like *how* or *why*—anything that requires the boss to form a complete sentence and explain himself. Bosses who wish to play the cards close to their vests answer questions with monosyllabic grunts. The locomotive and juvenile bosses dictate to their workhorses by issuing short orders with little or no explanation. Open-ended questions, by their very nature, prevent such secrecy.

We have entered the era of *glasnost*. The days of meek compliance because "the boss says so" are over. Some bosses believe that their position is reason enough for obedience to an order. Yet even caustic old locomotives can be softened up when they are drawn out by a good listener. This holds especially true for subordinates who know more about their jobs than the boss does. Questions from such savants are rarely ignored in the hope that some new kernel of wisdom may be unearthed. In the case of the political or juvenile boss, they may possibly be used to enhance their own image.

The more you get the boss talking, the more chance you have of making your two cents heard. Assertive listening, asking questions to direct the conversation, and making sure your ideas are heard will accelerate the process of taking control over your job.

Be Careful of "Constructive Criticism"

A good manager does not criticize subordinates. Instead they critique their work. Constructive criticism has a way of turning into to a one-sided attack when the locomotive and the disorganized incompetent are allowed to remain in control. Some bosses seek refuge in the label *constructive*, thinking this eliminates your ability to fend off their attack. Some begin such a "constructive" session by swinging the wrecking ball in your direction. You can forestall a boss who bares her fangs at you by reminding her of the favorable results other really constructive conversations had. This provides time to start setting ground rules for this session so it doesn't turn into a brawl.

Here's the message you want to instill in your boss regarding constructive criticism:

"I'll accept criticism when given in a helpful spirit. We'll talk about the job, instruction, supervision, and responsibilities. We won't talk about my self-worth as a human being or my intelligence. It's assumed that I am smart enough to do this job and that my integrity is not in question or I would not have been hired or allowed to remain here in the first place. Genuinely constructive criticism requires two-way communication. Where I feel there are things that both of us can do to improve, I'll let you know. Finally, this will be a calm and thought-provoking conversation. If you feel combative or antagonistic you don't really want a constructive conversation, you want to vent steam at someone."

The locomotive can be derailed by a subordinate who steadfastly sticks to these rules of survival. When you justly (and constructively) deserve criticism, accept it gracefully. Don't offer lame excuses or try to blame the boss. Most types of bosses, with the possible exception of the pleaser, view such contrary behavior as inflammatory. If you really don't know what you did wrong, ask the boss what you should have done. Determine how the alternative action would have helped the boss and the company. Learn from this conversation. Don't make the same mistake again. Many bosses feel that a miscue done once does not present a problem, but done again provides cause for concern regarding: (1) your interest in the job, (2) your interest in helping the boss, and (3) your intellectual capacity, your family heritage, and every other reason that can be conjured up for your stupidity.

If the session was beneficial to both of you (i.e., you directed the conversation and did not allow it to degenerate into a personal attack), say so. Thank the boss for thinking enough of you to point out these things. I have known bosses who admit that the employees they care about and believe have a future get bombarded with so-called constructive criticism. Those viewed as hopeless are ignored. Leave the door wide open for future conversations. Next time, you will be able to make known your constructive criticism of the boss.

LESSONS FOR THE BOSS

Control over your boss comes with letting him or her know how you want to be treated. Teach the boss what you want in terms of instruction, supervision, responsibilities, authority, and criticism. For most bosses and subordinates, communicating what you need in each of these areas comes bit by little bit.

Princess Rising Star, the juvenile boss, believes she has all the answers and, by virtue of her status as a superstar, even knows how to manage people. I. B. Meantuu, the locomotive, holds onto his authority and superiority as a drowning swimmer does a life preserver. Lame Duk, our political refugee from Peking, has little room for explanations that could lay bare his hidden agenda. Both pleasers and disorganized incompetents, however, can be the quickest learners, especially if you forcefully insist that their behavior makes you very unhappy or that they may share credit for a superior work product if they would just listen.

Instructions

Begin with the level of instruction needed to perform an assignment. Too little direction and the boss fails to tell you his requirements. Too much and the boss risks jeopardizing a subordinate's creativity. Alternative approaches to problem solving, which even the all-but-extinct Tyrantosaurus Wrecks (an ancient, rusting locomotive) may not have thought of, fall by the wayside. Failings by the boss at both ends of this spectrum are about evenly divided. The locomotive usually will beat subordinates over the head with instructions until the flame of innovation expires. Hurriup N. Wate, another disorganized incompetent, has so little time and knows so little about the assignment, that instructions, if given at all, are often wrong or incomplete.

Manage and direct the instruction conversation. Ask penetrating questions to fill any blanks that may be left. Stop the boss who tries to dot every *i* and cross every *t* for you. Think of the practical side of the assignment as instructions are given. Find out what information the boss has omitted. Often the boss will skip over significant facts or items necessary for the job either because they are obvious to him or because he doesn't know them. If you see this happening, regain control of the conversation. Political bosses, such as Lyan Lobby, who agree to unreasonable deadlines are adept at transferring responsibility for their errors to subordinates. When confronted with such a problem, raise the red flag. Make sure Lyan's time pressures, hidden agenda, or lack of knowledge about the job do not become your problem as well.

Excess instructions can flow from oversupervision to the point that the boss smothers you like an overstuffed pillow. Nobody likes having an overzealous supervisor breathing down their neck. Few things will ruin enthusiasm for a task faster than the boss constantly checking up. Further, most people learn best when they have to puzzle out a problem for themselves.

For the pleaser and DI bosses who oversupervise, a

verbal admonishment about time the boss wastes (both his and yours) in oversupervising often suffices. This should be given politely, firmly, and at the same time demonstrating that you have the situation under control. If the boss persists, something is wrong. Stop your work and confront the problem. Soon he'll get the message that his involvement actually retards progress. Search out the boss's problem. If you have been successful on other similar assignments, point them out. Find out if she thinks progress is too slow on the assignment. Does this present a problem in meeting the deadline? If so, what are you doing wrong? Perhaps you need help on the job (not more supervision, but real help). Whatever the problem, find it and fix it. Then suggest that now the boss can get on with doing her job rather than yours, too.

Responsibility + Authority = Trust

Control over your boss means that your responsibilities and authority to act are clearly understood. This includes the expected outcome of any assignment and the deadline for completion. You cannot play the game if you don't know the rules or the goals. From the start of the instruction session, make sure that both you and your boss agree exactly on your responsibilities. Also be clear on what special authorities you have to do the job. Such authorities might be hiring of personnel, purchase of materials, signature authorization, to name a few.

Beware of the boss who changes responsibilities and authorities on the fly. Tip Blabbermeister, the politician, often does this to cover his own mistakes. When this happens, be sure to let the boss know what he has done and how it affects your performance. When these ad hoc decisions impact your relations with others in the company, be sure they understand what happened and where you stand. For example, most companies hold check signing authority to be a coveted symbol of trust the firm places in an employee. If you are suddenly given temporary check signing authority (to pay for items purchased on your project, perhaps), do you think the original signatory will be upset? You bet! Further, if her boss is not your boss also, don't you think he will be hauled into the fray as well? Better to make sure your good name does not get smeared by an unthinking boss. When you get any new authority, think of how it will affect someone else, and deal with it before it becomes a cause célèbre.

Some people lack the ability to accept responsibility. Those who shove responsibility off on someone else (usually a boss or a subordinate) are "externalizing" their responsibility. If you are an externalizer, get over it. Once you have successfully fired your boss from your career, any mistakes that you make are purely yours. When you and your boss agree on your responsibilities for a task, accept them. No boss will trust someone who takes responsibility so lightly that she blames others for any failures that may result. If your boss does something that will cause you to fail in a responsibility, tell her while there's still time to fix it.

When you've obtained the responsibility and authority you need to act, you can be fairly sure you have earned a certain amount of trust from the boss. Treat the trust of your superiors as you would your most valued possession. A boss's trust goes deeper than simple confidence that a task will be done right the first time, completed when agreed upon, and with the amount of supervision you established at the outset. Real trust in someone extends to confidence in their reliability—reliability that the subordinate will safeguard the boss's reputation and keep him out of trouble.

Granted, for many bosses keeping them out of trouble requires both the patience of Job and the diplomatic skills of

Henry Kissinger. Thomas Paine said, "We must guard even our enemies against injustice." There exists a strong linkage between your boss's corporate image and yours. If your boss has a reputation for screwing up and many of the problems could have been fixed by subordinates who did not make the effort, your image becomes tarnished as well.

Furthermore, think about your boss's boss. This man or woman will approve the decision to promote you. When promoted, this person may become your boss. How much will he or she trust you if you have a reputation for not safeguarding your boss? Political bosses, like Tip Blabbermeister, want people working for them who will make them look good, not seize the opportunity to rip their carefully manicured image asunder.

Reward the Boss

Like a successful marriage, the relationship with your boss requires an enormous amount of communication to keep it healthy. Depending on the type of boss you have, communication may be just difficult, or it can seem impossible. Providing the boss with some sort of reward for doing what you wanted can start the ball rolling. Kenneth Blanchard and Spencer Johnson, in their best-selling book *The One Minute Manager* (William Morrow and Company, New York, NY), promote the idea of "catching the subordinate doing something right." This works equally well on bosses. Everyone (the tough locomotive and haughty juvenile included) likes to be told that their efforts have been noticed and appreciated.

Take care, however, not to become gushy and insincere. That can be worse than not giving a compliment at all. Simply tell the boss what he did that helped you (gave you the responsibility and authority to act, for a change) and how that made you feel. Point out any added benefits to the job this had. Give specific instances such as making your work go faster because you were able to circumvent some red tape. Let him know how you appreciate his confidence in you and that this, above all, is sacred (not quite, but you get the idea). Finally, simply thank him. He'll get the message.

Become the Expert

Perhaps the biggest help toward dominating your boss comes from knowing more about your job than he does. With such expertise automatically comes the deference one usually pays a superior. By definition, when you know more about the job than your boss, he no longer has the requisites to smother you. If you truly know more about the task, any instructions he may give you will be at best general in nature. You are in command.

How should you become the expert in your job? Mastery comes from two different directions. First from experience. You can absorb a certain amount of expertise simply by osmosis. How do you think the disorganized incompetent became a boss? Most likely by default because all the smart ones left the department for greener pastures. Gaining the requisite experience, however, takes too long. Your mental health and career may suffer unnecessarily in the interim, especially if your problem boss has pushed you to the point where you have made the decision to fire him or her from your career.

The second and fastest way to become the expert in the job requires plain hard work on your part. Take the time to puzzle out problems yourself. Read books on job-related subjects, and subscribe to magazines and newspapers that will keep you informed of the latest developments in your field. Of course this sounds elementary. Consider, however, the locomotive boss who thinks he knows it all. If he ever read a book or a magazine dealing with his job (doubtful), he would probably scoff at it as something from the ivory tower and never implement any of the ideas. The political boss probably doesn't read about his job either. He does not see job competence as a major rung on the corporate ladder. For him success comes from knowing the right people or having enough dirt on someone to use as leverage.

When you are able, begin writing about your job. Place your articles in the periodicals you have been reading. This is actually easier than you think. Professional magazines are always looking for fresh new ideas, especially from people currently involved in the field. Even more so, they love articles contributed by authors whom they don't have to pay. Prepare an outline of the article you want to write and send it to the editor of your target magazine. Follow this up with a phone call to personalize your idea. Sell yourself. When your article gets published, your status will be immediately upgraded. After several of your pieces have been published, begin giving speeches on the subjects you've written about. Before you know it, you've become an acknowledged industry expert. Simple.

Learn every facet of your job. Mastery of a job means you understand not only everything about what you personally do, but how you fit into the entire scheme of things. We had hoped for these things from your boss. Once she has been given the boot, however, the burden now falls on your shoulders. Expand your concept of the "work team" to include the rest of the company as well as your own department. Be aware of the sources of information on which you must rely to do your job. Watch for potential pitfalls from other departments (and help fix them if possible) that could damage your work product. Understand what happens to your work product after it leaves your department. What could you do to enhance the utility of your work for those who must deal with it later?

I had the pleasure of observing just such a self-made expert in one of the country's largest engineering and construction companies. One could tell that Ron was unusually technically competent just by observing how he worked with others. He was the junior member of a team run by a political boss. Ron knew everything about his job. He had a wonderful personal relationship with those who produced the information on which he relied to execute his job. He made it his business to know, and in many cases help, those who used his work product. Because of his engaging personality and his high degree of competence, people from other departments would consult Ron on questions concerning the department before consulting his boss (and then, only as a last resort). Soon Ron knew more about his job than did the boss. This was acknowledged in a humorous way at a staff meeting when Ron announced to the boss that he needed his help. The boss replied, "What, do you want me to help you lift something?" This broke the rest of the staff into laughter. More importantly, his boss publicly accepted that Ron had become his own master.

FEEDBACK: HAVE YOU TAUGHT THE RIGHT THINGS?

Remember Maggie the Scottie? She gave us feedback. Her behavior (requiring Nature's Miracle) said that we had taught her the wrong thing. Similarly, we need to be sure your boss understands what you want. Feedback from the boss can tell you which lessons must be repeated and which simply require reinforcement. Some bosses are reluctant to give feedback for fear of being wrong. If they compliment someone and later find that the success on which the were commenting was not the subordinate's doing, they risk embarrassment.

Careful observation will show you how effective your

lessons have been. If your boss still gives you needlessly detailed instructions that only serve to irritate and waste everyone's time, the message needs to be repeated. Don't be frustrated. My friends in the advertising business tell me that the average person needs to hear the same message many, many times before remembering it. Your boss has an even worse problem. She not only has to remember your message, she has to change a behavior that she developed over a period of time and that has brought her a measure of success.

Locomotive bosses can be the worst in terms of getting them to change. Because locomotives are often intimidating, it takes a lot of gumption to tell them they are wrong in the first place. Imagine what a personal threat it can be if you have to go to them again and again saying, "Look, Jack, don't you get it?" or put more bluntly, "What part of *NO* don't you understand?"

Christopher Hegarty, in his book *How to Manage Your Boss* (Ballantine Books, New York, NY), captured the locomotive's attitude toward criticism when he wrote, "I disagree with what you say, but I respect your right to be punished for it." Samuel Goldwyn (MGM Studios) was reputed to be a tough boss. The following quote was attributed to old Sam: "I don't want any yes-men around me. I want people who tell me the truth, even if it costs them their jobs."

Here are some tactics that will help you receive and give feedback with the boss:

The Boss's Image

There are two images of the boss: his own and the real one. Make sure of the accuracy of your perception of the boss. Does it jibe with that of the other subordinates? Turn off your emotions and make this an objective judgment. From childhood we are taught to think of all authority figures, bosses included, as being above reproach. Remove your boss from that pedestal.

The Boss's Self-perception

If the boss's self-image has little relation to reality, you need to tactfully set him straight. Otherwise he won't change the behaviors that you find so destructive. Talk to the boss. If he still oversupervises, find out what he thinks of a boss who oversupervises. Perhaps his own boss does this. Draw him out by asking open-ended questions. How does he feel when his own boss rides him like a rodeo cowboy? Does it add to his own productivity? Maybe what appears as oversupervision to you simply means a great interest in your success to the boss.

Keep the Boss from Becoming Defensive

When eliciting feedback from the boss, keep it from appearing judgmental. Although placing the boss in a defensive position may make you feel good, it doesn't help to discover the problem. Observations that begin as statements such as, "When you do _____ , I feel _____ ", help to draw out the boss's reasoning. Reinforce the boss by reminding him of the previous lessons you've tried to teach him. Do this in a manner that does not scold but rather lets him know that you both really need his behavior to change.

If the boss clams up you can almost force him to talk with you by repeating back what you thought he has said or feels. Often this will be wrong. That's OK. The boss will correct you, and the conversation will continue to flow.

You must receive and give feedback to be sure the boss understands what you want. Do not water down the feedback you give your boss or accept feedback that you know to be short of the truth. Pleaser bosses are afraid to give complete and honest feedback to subordinates. Some male bosses such as Tyrantosaurus Wrecks (undoubtedly with roots from prehistoric times) still have the image of female workers as somehow weaker than their male counterparts. This can greatly restrain an honest give-and-take in the feedback process. Make sure you communicate that you can take well-founded, constructive criticism, you won't become irritated and storm out before he can explain, you are very interested and will be a receptive listener, and that you care what he thinks.

Don't back off in demanding feedback if your lessons go unheeded. Doing so only imperils your career.

THE HOOK

Like most of us, bosses are interested in what's in it for them. Self-interest can be a powerful hook when used to dominate your boss. Neither the juvenile nor the political boss will assist you unless he can be shown that his own ambitions will be furthered. The disorganized incompetent will continue to demand to approve every decision unless you demonstrate that he will gain more by surrendering some authority. The locomotive has to be assured that the need for his experience and leadership will be enhanced if he reduces supervision to the bare essentials. Trying to convince him that overly detailed assignment instructions displease you will be heard about as well as a whisper in a hurricane. Such a suggestion, however, will get the attention of the pleaser boss.

Juvenile and political bosses are motivated by one thing: their personal advancement. When used properly, the "theory of succession" can be a persuasive motivator. The theory of succession means that your boss can't move up unless there exists an acceptable candidate to take his or her place. Here, logic comes into play. You want a crack at becoming the boss's successor. How can you be viewed as a potential candidate unless you are allowed to:

- Figure out the approach to assignments yourself and put your own background and knowledge into their execution;
- Stop relying on the boss to supervise every step of every task you do;
- Accept responsibility for completion of assignments without relying on the boss;
- Receive the authority to do whatever it takes to complete an assignment.

Realistically the theory of succession holds little consequence for the locomotive boss whose hopes for advancement became extinct long ago. It does work, however, on juvenile, political, and pleaser bosses.

Here is another hook called the mirror effect. This means that a group of self-reliant, happy subordinates reflects back favorably on the boss. Imagine how the pleaser would beam if his boss remarked how proud he is that the pleaser's employees seem to be developing, are happy, costly turnover is below company average, and his department has become a veritable talent pool from which other areas of the company can draw seasoned competent personnel. Such accolades do not come to bosses who are allowed to crush creativity with absurdly detailed instructions, pulverize individuality by oversupervising, and extinguish professional growth by withholding responsibility and authority.

LAST RESORT: THE THREAT

Threats of adverse action should be used only as a last resort. Never threaten your boss unless you are prepared to carry it out. There are only two threats that work. Unfortunately both have to do with leaving. You can threaten to leave the company and go to a competitor, or you can threaten to request a transfer to another department. Your reasons (overbearing and stifling boss, limited growth due to zero responsibility and authority) reflect very harshly on your boss. Threats of disassociation can be doubly effective if you have made yourself the expert in your job and you have developed a better working relationship with other departments and their heads than has your boss.

If you take this drastic action, deal from a position of strength. Have another job offer in hand from a firm you would be happy to work for before you voice your threat (you may be invited by your boss to accept the offer). If your boss refuses to see your point and declines to pay attention, you are better off away from him or her anyway.

Threatening to leave means that you have failed to fire your boss. Instead, you must start over with a new boss and a new set of problems. If you take this action, get to know all the potential pitfalls of working for your new boss before you accept the offer. Identify what type of boss he or she will be. Let him know in no uncertain terms why you had to leave your old boss and observe closely how he responds. Ask if he has had similar experiences and how he handled them. Talk with some of his subordinates privately. Most employers will be happy to spend this kind of time with someone in whom they are truly interested. Do not step from the frying pan into the fire.

Many people doggedly endure the abuses of their boss. Better the devil they know than one they don't. Nonsense. If you have made a genuine effort to communicate to your boss how you are to be treated and she still remains inflexible, there is no shame in admitting defeat. Don't procrastinate in making your decision. A problem boss creates career problems and makes for an unhappy personal life as well. Move just as fast as you can, and get on with the rest of your life.

INSTRUCTIONS TO DOMINATE YOUR BOSS

1. Become the expert in your job

  A. "Run for office" by:
    1. publishing articles,
    2. giving speeches.
  B. Understand the entire process of which your job is but one part.
  C. Establish excellent working relationships with other departments and bosses.

2. Soften up the boss

  A. Make sure the boss's self-image is based in reality.
  B. Identify the hook and set it.

3. Institute ground rules

  A. Construct your autonomy by:
    1. identifying work instructions,
    2. establishing the level of supervision needed.
  B. Obtain authority to act.
  C. Accept responsibility for success and failure.
  D. Determine acceptable criticism.

4. Reinforce good behavior

  A. Use praise, compliments, and rewards.
  B. Cement continued good behavior.
  C. Use feedback.

IV

Hold Your Boss's Feet to the Fire: Ensuring Accountability

Most of us have wondered just how our boss actually championed our cause when thrashing out raises and bonuses with his or her own boss. Actions replace rhetoric and promises, or as a bumper sticker at the Indianapolis Motor Speedway said, "When the green flag drops, the bullshit stops." Let's see how one person scored on this all-important test:

"John, as Cathy's boss, it's my responsibility to stick up for her when we allocate bonuses. She is one of our most creative people. The firm owes much of its reputation to her kitchen-design skills. Did I tell you we had a screaming 'shoutfest' after last year's meager bonus? Later SHE described what performance she thought would rate her as a huge success in this firm. She then told me what type of bonus would be appropriate if she met her goals. I agreed. She even wrote me a memo outlining our conversation. Throughout the year, every so often, Cathy reminded me of her progress and that she expected me to fulfill my part of our agreement come bonus time. Cathy has exceeded each one of those goals. John, we both owe her big time, and I won't back down."

Cathy has indeed made her boss accountable for her own behavior. Let's analyze what Cathy did to cause her boss to feel such a strong commitment:

1. *First*: Cathy let her boss know in clear terms that last year's bonus did not cut it.
2. *Second*: She took the offensive and removed goals and rewards from her boss's control by setting them herself.
3. *Third*: Once the goals and rewards were established, Cathy put them in writing.
4. *Fourth*: She gained and kept her boss's commitment.

Cathy followed these four steps and obtained what she had bargained for with her boss. She landed an added benefit when her boss's boss heard of her success, further lessening the influence of her immediate supervisor. For most of us, holding the boss answerable for actions affecting our career represents a new approach. Bosses would like us to think that they know best when it comes to the company and its employees. Nonsense. As usually happens, the weaker the boss, the more steadfastly they believe this. Princess Rising Star, the juvenile boss, allows little room for questions, afraid that her authority will be challenged. Many management blunders go unrecognized because subordinates are afraid to question the boss's authority or the boss is simply too inept to listen. As in the case with the space shuttle *Challenger*, several engineers vigorously recommended against launch. To the later horror of the world, they were overruled by bosses whose agenda allegedly included something other than the primary mission of a safe launch.

Employees who fail to hold their reckless or incompetent bosses accountable for their actions risk allowing otherwise good careers to go astray. Even the federal government has recognized the importance of accountability by enacting a whistle-blowing statute to protect employees who criticize their bosses.

While techniques and approaches vary with different types of bosses and your particular work situation, the concept is universal. The four steps to hold your boss's feet to the fire are:

1. Establish communication

In our example, Cathy told her boss of her disappointment. It never pays to suffer silently. Confront the problem and give good reasons why you object. Failure to establish ground rules for your boss's behavior invites treatment as a floor mat. When the going gets tough and a boss has to decide between disappointing someone who will meekly accept it or someone who the boss knows will not sit still for such drivel, who gets the shaft? Business relationships, like marriages, rely on communication to survive.

2. Identify goals and rewards

Cathy insisted that her boss work with her to correct the problem. Hard work and rewards are an everyday part of the business world. Your boss must, however, agree with the goals and commit to the rewards. Participative conversations gain this commitment best. When the boss contributes to the dialogue (without being allowed to dictate as the locomotive and juvenile will try), the commitment will be that much greater for both of you.

3. Put it in writing

Writing adds further credence that you are serious about the decisions made during the goal/reward discussion. Additionally, such an instrument will later be used for guidance in evaluating performance and determining rewards. For bosses reluctant to put anything potentially incriminating in writing (Lyan Lobby, the political boss, has been reputed to use disappearing ink!), this document measures the level of commitment. A boss who doesn't want a written record of what was committed to you probably has little intent to honor the agreement.

4. Periodic reinforcement

Everyone needs to be reminded of promises or commitments they have made. Informal progress reports imply that you are doing your part and that you expect your boss to do his. When done on a regular and informal basis, your boss will be kept informed on progress toward your goals.

GOALS OF ACCOUNTABILITY

Responsible bosses feel accountable to subordinates for their actions. Such bonding comes in several important forms. First, bosses must be made to feel that your success depends on them in some significant way. I. B. Meantuu, the bullet train, obviously feels little allegiance when he says, "I'll give him just enough rope to hang himself."

Second, the boss must understand that you are serious about the goals and rewards on which you both agree. When you make or exceed your goals, your boss will be expected to fulfill her end of the deal. This can be most important when working for a politician or a pleaser. These defective personality types may make an agreement to appease you without realizing the political implications that may cause them to renege later. Additionally, watch out for the boss who thinks either your goals are unattainable and he will be off the hook or the time frame is so far in the future that he can conveniently forget the original discussion. Bosses who view meetings scheduled for next week as "a lifetime away" are particularly dangerous in this regard.

A third objective of making your boss accountable has to do with your boss blowing your horn for you. In the example, Cathy's boss told her own boss that Cathy is "one of our most creative people." Finally, she closed the sale saying, "The firms owes much of its reputation to her kitchen-design skills." In a real sense, her boss indirectly blew her own horn while trumpeting Cathy's success. She felt in some way at least partially responsible. This commitment to Cathy, and the boss's participation in her success, made it very easy to tell her own boss about her personnel-development skills.

Employees who allow their boss to buckle under pressure fail the fourth goal of accountability. Political pressures may cause your boss to weaken at the last split second unless you constantly reinforce your boss's obligation to you. If you have correctly established accountability, your boss will understand that unhappy consequences are sure to follow if he fails you (translated: "Hold your boss's feet to the fire.").

The success our example designer enjoyed with her boss came as no accident. Such successes are the result of a long-term, deliberate effort extended to ensure a favorable outcome. To some, this may seem manipulative. On the contrary, few processes in business are as straightforward. The boss, like everyone, must be nurtured and receive periodic reinforcement along with progress reports. It should never come as a surprise that a boss's protégé has in fact succeeded in meeting his or her goals and the time has come to pay the piper.

Meeting with Your Boss

The first step in making your boss accountable calls for a formal meeting. This meeting occurs only once.

Goals, performance standards, and rewards get hammered out here. You must control this meeting as much as possible. After all, you decided when you fired your boss that you are the best person to define such important items in your career.

SET THE STAGE

Setting the stage involves a bit of common sense. First, choose the right time for the meeting. Make sure both you and your boss will have enough time to complete the task without being disturbed. Try to schedule the meeting during a time when there are no important deadlines preoccupying you both. If possible, have your meeting shortly after a success you've each enjoyed. Finally, don't be afraid to reschedule the meeting if you see the timing is not right.

Be sure the boss understands the purpose of the meeting. Do not schedule the meeting through the boss's secretary. Doing this places you at risk of damage from the secretary. He or she may forget to tell the boss the purpose of the meeting or get the message garbled. Neither should you send the boss a memo requesting a meeting. You would not appreciate receiving a cold note announcing a "performance review" meeting. Neither would your boss. Invite him in person, tell him the subject matter of the meeting (so he can prepare), and set a definite time and date.

Next, do not minimize the importance of the meeting. Some people when asked, "What's this all about?", intimate that it's no biggie. Nonsense. This is a very big deal. Don't minimize its importance, and don't back down from insisting on a face-to-face meeting. If the boss does not think it's important to you, it's certainly not going to be important to him. Before you know it, you will be superseded by something "really important."

Have the meeting on your own turf, preferably in your own office. There, you are in control. If you don't have an office or for whatever reason your space is not appropriate, have the meeting in a neutral area; any place but your boss's office. You need to be in control, not your boss.

Written Agenda

Prepare a written agenda of the points your meeting should cover. Agendas are helpful, especially if you are new to asserting control. Additionally, such preparation places you in authority from the start, lets your boss know that you are serious about this and have come prepared. Your agenda should include at least the following points:

- Explanation of the purpose of the meeting and expected results;
- Reasons you must take charge of your goals;
- Establishment of goals;
- Establishment of rewards;
- Expectations of mutual performance.

Be certain that you maintain enough control of the conversation that these points are clearly made.

Definitely take notes. You both want to remember each point made during the meeting.

Goals

When considering your goals, choose them carefully. Ask yourself three questions about the goals you select:

- Do they truly help the company?
- Are they viewed as important to you, your boss, and his boss?
- Can achievement of these goals help justify your rewards?

Sell the boss on the project. Describe the benefits of your goals for the company as well as for your boss. Goals should be as specific as possible to avoid future disputes as to exact meanings. A good example of a specific goal for the treasurer of a company would be to decrease the average balance needed in the checking account from $200,000 to $100,000. Assuming this goal does not conflict with covenants and restrictions of lending agreements, it will save the company money because funds sitting in the checking account generally do not draw interest.

The benefits of your goals should be noted in quantitative terms, if possible. Using our example of the treasurer, this is easy: $200,000 less $100,000 equals $100,000 available to reduce the bank line borrowing that carries an interest rate of ten percent for one year, yields a $10,000 benefit.

Notice and concentrate on the kind of boss you have during goal setting. Lyan Lobby, the politician, may view achievement of these goals as an opportunity to safely score some points on something politically risky. Don't let him send you to the gallows without first understanding the risks you are undertaking on his behalf. Imagonna Grabontoitz, the disorganized incompetent, may look upon achieving these goals as helping him out of a jam that either he can't do or can't find the time to do. Do not allow Imagonna to look good at your expense. Letsall Getalong, the pleaser, may agree with everything you say just to mollify you. Be careful here, too. You want Getalong's commitment, not some meaningless babble to which he has no intention of being held accountable. Guard against I. B. Meantuu, the locomotive, as well. He may allow you to establish a goal, knowing it to be well beyond your capacity to reach, just to see you fail while enhancing his superiority.

Define Success

Have a firm concept of how your success will be judged. When you reach your goals, there should be no possibility of dispute that you did indeed achieve what you said you would. This only frustrates you and your boss. In the end it counts as a failure. Performance standards must be as well-defined as the actual goal. Continuing with our treasurer example, success could be determined by review of the account analysis statement received from the bank at the end of the year. On this statement appears the average balance in the checking account. Bingo. Here lies undisputable proof of the treasurer's achievement. Even the most obtuse bosses cannot successfully argue against independent verification of a subordinate's success.

There should also be some room for error when defining success. If you set out six goals and meet the five most important but fall short on the last, what does that mean in terms of your reward? Do not place your boss in the overbearing position of being judge and jury after the fact. Additionally, often there are circumstances truly beyond your control (such as your boss's ineptitude) that may adversely affect your success. Be sure such eventualities are considered when defining success.

Establish Rewards

Once the goals and standards of performance are defined, describe what you want in return for doing all these great things. You and your boss must be in mutual agreement on these rewards. Rewards should be precise, again to avoid possibility of misunderstanding. Make sure your boss has the authority to grant each reward. If a reward appears beyond your boss's authority, ask him to go to his boss or the person who does have authority and gain a commitment.

This avoids confusion and disappointment later. Beware again of the pleaser who agrees to anything and the disorganized incompetent who thinks he has the authority to grant a reward but in fact does not.

Think about what exactly your rewards should be and include them in your agenda outline. Rewards come in many forms. Cash bonuses are nice. Most people welcome an extra week of vacation. Salary raises are often appropriate. Advancement to a specific position demonstrates a commitment to your career and the company. Company cars are useful perks, as are expense accounts, use of the company country club, additional life insurance, etc. Be creative. The rewards you establish will greatly influence your motivation and your ultimate success.

Commitment and Reinforcement

If your boss has gone along with you to this point, you are doing a great job. Provided that the boss has actively participated in this project, he or she should feel a certain amount of responsibility for its success. Now, reduce the session to writing. The written record of your agreement becomes the first step in firming up your boss's commitment. Additionally, it reinforces the seriousness of the exercise you both completed. This document also becomes the blueprint to achieve your goals. Get your boss to carefully review it and make any changes necessary. Except under special circumstances, do not ask for your boss's signature agreeing to the goals and rewards. He probably does an adequate job of insulting his personal integrity without your help.

Now comes periodic reinforcement. Let the boss know how you are doing on your goals. You want to strengthen the idea that you intend to reach each goal and be rewarded for doing so. Periodic reinforcement also provides a forum for both of you to make mid-course corrections in either goals, success definitions, or reward structures. Be careful, however, not to overdo the reinforcement. It should be done casually, without formality. You don't want to rub your boss's nose in the fact that you've replaced his traditional role, nor do you want to appear insecure. Periodic reinforcement can be done at a luncheon, for example, or in the car on the way to a client's office. Also, don't be afraid to ask for help if you need it. Your boss may be able to help you hit your targets, and this will strengthen his commitment to your success. Be careful, however, that your boss's assistance does not hinder the effort. Remember, an incompetent boss was probably a marginal worker. That kind of help you don't need.

As long as you correctly reinforce the goals and rewards, it should be clear that you hold your boss accountable for his actions. If you suspect otherwise, unearth the problem and correct it as soon as possible. Do not give your boss the opportunity to become weak at the last instant (as the pleaser and the disorganized incompetent may tend to do in the face of adversity). Holding your boss's feet to the fire reminds him of WHAT you expect to do and that you will INSIST he deliver on his promises.

PUT THEORY INTO PRACTICE

So much for the theory of gaining your boss's commitment and helping you reach your goals. All of the above will be just an academic exercise if you don't perform. Here are some ways to ensure that you achieve your goals:

Set Priorities

Which goal should you tackle first? Hopefully, you have several tasks that can be done simultaneously. Much as the engineers develop a critical path for a construction project, you should develop your own strategy to hit your targets within the specified time. The first project should be chosen because it can be completed quickly and will have an impact on your department. You want to begin with a quick success to show your boss that not only do you intend to succeed, you have, in fact, begun. Even though the first project may not be the most important, its planning, execution, success, and speed of delivery will set the tone for the rest of your goals. Ideally the first task should be able to be completed within one week. Upon completion, let the boss know of your success. No one will tout your successes but you, whereas everyone will trumpet your failures.

Once you put the first task to bed, determine the ones that can be done simultaneously and find out if some must be completed before others can begin. If some tasks must follow others, carefully establish the order. Do not make yourself wait to complete one project because its predecessor task has yet to be completed. When faced with a choice, select the project that can be done the fastest and has the greatest benefit to your department and/or the company.

Work Efficiently and Effectively

Efficiency and effectiveness go hand in hand but do not mean exactly the same thing. In the second chapter, we discussed the difference between working efficiently and effectively. Efficiency means that you do things right the first time. Your work does not have to come to a grinding halt because you made a mistake. The saying that there never seems to be time to do it right but always time to do it again may be true for much of the work force, but not for you.

Effectiveness means that as your own boss you not only

do your job right, but you also do the right THINGS to meet your goals. In other words, don't waste time pursuing dead ends or doing things that will not help accomplish the task at hand. Become notorious for achieving what you set out to do.

Cross Departmental Lines

You cannot become an expert in your job without being aware of how your task got to you and what happens to it after it leaves your department. You should know the people in the departments both before your task and after, what they do, their work problems, their capabilities, and their resources. Such knowledge allows your influence to expand and will likely benefit you.

I once knew of a supervisor in the collections division of a large credit card company. After he fired his boss and assumed that role himself, he began to cross departmental lines. First he went to the supervisor of the group that identified the delinquent accounts and sent them to his department for collection. He and the supervisor were able to devise a way to accurately predict how many accounts would be rolling into his area three months in advance. It turned out that this helped him tremendously in meeting his staffing goals.

Next he moved two departments down the line into the treasurer's department. The treasurer had difficulty predicting cash flow because results of the collections efforts were unpredictable. As it turned out, the collections operation closely monitored its results and reported them periodically, but not to the treasurer. With some simple formatting changes in the collections results reports, the treasurer greatly reduced the amount of cash cushion he needed in the checking account. This allowed the company to repay some debt and reduce its interest expense. More important from the employee's standpoint, the supervisor made a corporate friend outside his immediate department. Such successful relationships can help broaden your influence and make you less dependent on the favorable opinion of your immediate boss.

Avoid "Analysis Paralysis"

Few things irritate both bosses and subordinates more than the inability to make a decision. If you see this as an unproductive drain on your time caused by an inept dodo, you are right. Don't be guilty of the same thing. If you do not make your own decisions, someone, like your boss, will make them for you. If this happens too often, whatever ground you gained from establishing a goal-and-reward system will soon be negated.

Your decision process should involve the following:

- Identify the problem;
- Identify the options under debate;
- Project the results of each alternative if implemented. Be sure to extend the results as far into the firm as possible so you don't do something that helps you but damages another department;
- Make the decision and implement it.

Do not keep recycling this process to avoid committing yourself. Often there exists no best answer to a problem. When that happens, choose the best solution you can using your best judgment, and be done with it. Take responsibility, and don't be afraid to fail. One of the most successful products, the yellow, gummed Post-it notepad, now universally in use, came about as the result of a failure. The gum used as the adhesive on these handy memo slips began life on the drawing board as super glue. When it became obvious that it didn't work, some enterprising person thought to put it on paper for use as a temporary note.

Stop Watching the Clock

Remember, if you have made it this far, you are well on your way to becoming your own boss. Such people have an intense commitment to success—so intense, in fact, that they do not measure the workday in a standard eight hours. If it takes working later than usual or on weekends to accomplish your goals, then do it.

Progress Rewards

Some people know themselves so well they understand their need for progress or interim rewards to keep going through a long grind. If you find yourself working significantly harder than usual at your job and you are achieving noticeable success, consider an interim reward. Of course, it would be best if the reward structure already provided for this. Demonstrate some of the success you have had in achieving your goals before they are complete. Chances are that your boss will have noticed your increased activity and already be aware of your successes. If you need an advance on the reward to maintain your commitment, then ask for it. If you are not permitted an advance on your reward, it may be an indication of future difficulty in getting the entire reward. Correction of the problem now, prior to your deadline, can save a lot of anguish later.

The steps detailed above are summarized in the following Checklist for Developing Accountability:

CHECKLIST FOR DEVELOPING ACCOUNTABILITY

Use this list to be sure you have set the stage and created a commitment on the part of your boss.

1. Prepare for the goal-setting meeting

Develop an effective agenda that details the goals, the performance standards, and the rewards you want.

2. Set the stage and stack the deck

Plan the meeting at the most advantageous time and location.

3. Control the meeting

Accomplish what you need to during the meeting. Do not let the conversation stray from your purpose. Retain control of the agenda. Take notes to be sure of the accuracy of your recollection later.

4. Get your boss's commitment

This begins with your boss's acceptance of the written record of the meeting. Use progress reports and requests for help to periodically reinforce commitment.

5. Manage yourself

It is true that most of us hold ourselves to a higher standard than do our bosses. Be sure that this applies to you. Average performance doesn't set you above anyone but the mediocre. Make your own decisions or someone will make them for you. Do the right things on the job and work effectively. Work efficiently by doing things right the first time. When in doubt, use your best judgment. Avoid analysis paralysis. Don't be afraid to venture out of your own department; you'll be surprised how much others can help you and you can help others.

6. Give your boss a final pep talk

Start shortly before your boss will have to begin granting your rewards. Strengthen his or her commitment to you and your successful achievement of mutually established goals. Let there be no doubt that you have succeeded and that the benefits to your boss and the company as a result of your efforts are worthwhile. When it comes time to actually grant your rewards, the boss's actions should come as no surprise.

The prior four chapters have dealt with the principles and objectives of firing your boss. We identified the various boss types, learned the principles of self-supervision, the necessity for dominating the boss, and the importance of accountability. The next four chapters deal with the actual mechanics of dependence, authority, resources, and leadership.

V

One for the Money: Using Your Boss's Dependence to Liberate Yourself

"When it comes to our shipping schedules, Jim is the authority. If it moves throughout our system and needs to be there on time, I know Jim will get the job done with no excuses. It doesn't bother me being so dependent on one person, not with Jim's reliability. Used to be I had to do everything myself. Now I don't know what I would do without him. As a matter of fact, I've decided to expand Jim's responsibility to include raw-material inventory. If he can do with that mess what he did with scheduling, I can retire."

We are taught from elementary school never to question the teacher's authority. Throughout most of the first twenty years of our lives we were rewarded for respecting whatever the person in charge did, regardless of whether it was right or wrong. The Establishment conspired to make us compliant. Worse, our independent spirit was crushed.

Blind acceptance of authority naturally transfers itself to the workplace. If the boss says to wait on a decision until he gets time to review it, we wait. If the boss insists on signing authorizations to request materials that are obviously needed, the job lingers. Most of us find comfort and security in a "follow the herd" mentality. Few dare to seize the initiative and circumvent that time-honored tradition of succumbing to authority.

Where does dependence on an inept boss lead us? Frustrated, behind in our work, taking our personal time to make up for the inefficiencies of a boss who views overtime (especially for salaried employees) as a privilege, symbolic of how important you are to the company. The hazards of remaining dependent on an inept boss include:

- Wasting time waiting for the boss's approval of decisions that you should make yourself;
- Allowing the timeliness of your work to be ruined by a procrastinating dullard who often has a terminal case of analysis paralysis;
- Permitting the sparkle of your work to become tarnished by an incapable dolt who insists on personally presenting the department's work to her superiors.

To succeed in firing the boss from your career, you must regain your independence. When done correctly, the ineffectual boss welcomes dependence on a highly skilled and well-regarded subordinate. Imagonna Grabontoitz, the disorganized incompetent boss featured in the example at the beginning of the chapter, decides to add to Jim's responsibilities and makes him head of a small department. Most likely this idea came from Jim as well.

OBJECTIVES OF DEPENDENCE

Subordinates who make the boss dependent on them sharply reduce the negative influences an unfit boss can create. When you reverse superior/subordinate dependence, the balance of power over your career shifts from the boss to you. The boss must be sucked gradually into the quicksand of dependence until it becomes a natural part of business life and he's in too deep to get out even if he wanted to. The boss should be made to depend on you for such things as:

- Technical know-how;
- Keeping the boss out of trouble;
- Knowing just who to ask for special favors and how to slash through red tape;
- Acting as a reliable accurate sounding board.

Dependency on you for any one or all of these things increases the hold you have over your own destiny.

Leverage created by a dependent boss figures into most business decisions affecting you. Bosses who rely on a valued subordinate listen all the more carefully when depth of instruction, amount of supervision, responsibility, and authority are brought up. Further, when promotions are discussed, those employees who have made themselves so obviously valued are the first to be snapped up by other department heads. At the very least, the largest raises go to those who provide the most value to the company. Value translates directly to the level of trust and dependence the boss has in you.

DEPENDENCY AND TYPES OF BOSSES

The type of boss you have will dictate the amount of dependency you can create. Some bosses, such as Letsall Getalong, the complaint pleaser, can be very easy to turn the tables on. For others, such as the disorganized incompetent, failure to gain the upper hand can mean that his ineffectiveness becomes yours.

Political bosses, such as Lyan Lobby, spend a lot of time "working the crowd" and less time practicing good management. They often welcome someone on whom they can count to run the shop while out on a junket. Locomotive and juvenile bosses resist becoming dependent more than any other boss type. These bosses painstakingly guard their authority and believe that they know more than you do (sometimes true). Further, many have themselves succeeded in making their own bosses dependent on them.

Here's how to deal with the particular type of boss you may have.

Disorganized Incompetent

Danger from the DI comes in the form of their instability. Most DIs create a crisis atmosphere, where everyone works under a perpetual cloud of impending doom. The crises are usually created by DIs such as Hurriup N. Wate, who proudly states that she thrives under pressure and those who can't take it have no business in the "real world."

Everyone's ability to deal productively with pressure differs. Professors Yerkes and Dodson researched the point at which additional pressure begins to deteriorate performance. They formulated the Yerkes–Dodson Law of Stress, which describes stress and its effects in a mathematical formula. This law states that there exists a bell-shaped curve, which plots performance against stress. The peak of the bell curve shows top performance at a midpoint of pressure. Further pressure exerted beyond the optimum makes performance decline.

The DI tends to shoot from the hip, especially when committing to deadlines for the department. Due to Wate's notoriously bad working relationships with her peers, assistance from other departments never emerges. Further, because Wate must work extraordinarily long hours to compensate for her inefficiency, her staff must also. When the department misses deadlines, at the very least, the resulting taint will rub off on you.

To the DI, everything is urgent. "The difference between urgent and important is the difference between thoughtfulness and panic," says the article entitled "Managing Without Managers" by Richard Semler (*Harvard Business Review*, October 1989). DIs, such as Hurriup N. Wate, favor panic.

Dependence on a capable subordinate for key tasks in the department are necessary to keep the boss from running (and ruining) your life. For example, instead of letting a DI such as Imagonna Grabontoitz continue to schedule jobs with unrealistic deadlines, transfer that responsibility to someone who understands the work load.

Imagonna will allow his ridiculously crowded schedule to fill the void and probably won't even notice that he was spun out of the scheduling loop. The impact on your life will be remarkable. You can now control the deadlines that were impossible earlier. Your reputation as a "can-do" manager will grow as you develop a track record of tasks successfully completed. Your word will become trusted, rather than doubted like that of Grabontoitz.

Finally, because you have become the scheduling expert, not only has Imagonna become dependent on your abilities, so has the rest of the firm. As dependence on you grows, so will the amount of clout you can bring to bear on your boss. With such recognition comes a further decrease in the influence the DI has over your career.

Political Boss

When you know your job so thoroughly that your boss could never hope to possess your knowledge with all the other things he or she has to do, the inclination to publicly relinquish that responsibility takes over. After all, an inept politician like Lyan Lobby does not want to be at risk for something over which he has little control.

Political bosses are among the easiest to make dependent. Their instinct for self-preservation often allows you to step in and grab the reins. Politicians are more easily convinced to depend on someone for technical knowledge. The details of most projects require time and concentration to understand. Neither of these two attributes are strengths of the politician. Furthermore, when an element of risk can be introduced, the politico will make every effort to insulate himself.

Locomotive Boss

Because he uses brute force to manage his subjects and because he knows more about the job than any of his counterparts, creating an element of dependency can be difficult when facing an oncoming locomotive. These types of bosses do, however, have a soft spot for subordinates who make it known they want to learn from the master. Because locomotives have little upward mobility, they derive satisfaction from the job in two ways: seeing the fruits of their labors, and watching protégés prosper. You can make the boss dependent on you for both of these psychological needs. Here's how to deal with the locomotive:

First, nothing can be so irritating as someone who thinks she knows it all—especially to those of us who really do! The locomotive boss was there before you arrived and will probably still be there after you leave. Locomotives like I. B. Meantuu have little patience for someone viewed as unseasoned, untried, and wet behind the ears. The more such a subordinate tries to prove she has something to offer, the more Meantuu will resist. You don't want to be in a position of the boss withholding necessary advice just to see you fail. A dyed-in-the-wool locomotive will do just that to confirm his superiority.

On the other hand, you can gain a great deal from the boss's experience and inside knowledge of the company. Become his star student. Do not let his overbearing manner and impatience at small errors get to you. That's just his way of keeping young upstarts in their places. Give him what his own career has not provided: accolades and thanks for a job well done. In your case, the job happens to be moving you farther along on your career path. This is not being manipulative. It simply gives someone who probably hasn't seen it in a while a solid dose of simple human kindness. The more he responds, the easier it becomes to give.

When the locomotive boss sees that his efforts are not wasted, that you have indeed listened to his teachings and have succeeded as a result, you will become his compatriot. The natural tendency of the locomotive to guard authority and responsibilities will begin to crumble as he seeks additional confirmation of his abilities as a teacher. Rather than remain someone to be distrusted, you have become a source of pride. Your successes become the boss's, too. Don't forget it, and make sure the boss knows how much you appreciate his help.

As you assume more responsibility and are given more authority, the locomotive boss will become dependent on you for your job skills rather than simply as a testimonial to his own abilities. When this occurs you have truly made the boss dependent on you both as a person and for your unique abilities.

Juvenile Boss

The juvenile boss has many of the same attributes as the locomotive. They are both authoritarian, and both have all the answers. Each zealously guards his authority and is reluctant to delegate responsibilities. The difference, however, comes from the juvenile's lack of experience. Rather than rising through the ranks, the juvenile was quickly promoted to prominence by sheer technical ability. Among today's high-technology companies, juvenile bosses are treated as royalty.

Not being familiar with management, the juvenile, such as Princess Rising Star, will revert back to what she does best—your job. Your skill at keeping the boss from doing your work, rather than her own, can be the greatest help you can give. Teaching your boss how to manage and lead will help you not only dominate the boss, but create a certain amount of dependence as well.

The juvenile boss, with your help, will continue to rise. With the closeness generated by her dependence on your contacts and patience with her lack of managerial abilities, you can ride up with her. Perhaps you can take her place when she advances to the next rung. Even better, perhaps you can move up with her.

Pleaser

Pleasers are always trying to calm the turbulence that has become a natural part of most businesses. Letsall Getalong, an infamous pleaser, depends on his subordinates not to rock the boat. Getalong views disagreement as equivalent to civil disobedience. You must couch your disagreement with him in a manner that keeps it professional rather than unruly.

To avoid compromising your values as well as your image of being honest, straightforward, and self-sufficient, you must assert your ideas and requirements, even though someone else may disagree. This sometimes begs for confrontation and may not endear you to the pleaser.

About the best a dependent pleaser can hope for in a subordinate is one who will not unfairly criticize him—

someone on whom he can count not to be argumentative just to rattle his chain. Because your objective with the pleaser includes creating as much distance as possible from him, it will be difficult to vociferously back him in his compromises. Yet, when you can support your pleaser boss, you should do it enthusiastically and with conviction. After all, part of the image you need to create includes loyalty.

METHODS TO CREATE DEPENDENCE

Self-interest

Saul W. Gellerman, in his book *Motivation and Productivity* (American Management Association, Inc., Vail-Ballou Press, 1963), described the theory of "psychological advantage." Simply stated this theory says that people constantly seek to serve their own self-interests. Hardly earthshaking. You can make this simplistic theory work for you by identifying what self-interest motivates your boss, then deliver it.

Some key self-interest motivators for our five boss types follow:

- Locomotive: esteem and need to be needed;
- Juvenile: upward mobility;
- Disorganized incompetent: short-term survival;
- Pleaser: group cohesiveness;
- Political: one-upmanship.

Some bosses, especially locomotives such as I. B. Meantuu, count on reinforcement of their superiority from subordinates. Depending on how successful this type of boss views his career, the more helpful his attitude will be toward your attempts to learn from him. Successful bosses tend to adopt an encouraging attitude toward subordinates. Bosses who view their careers as unsuccessful fear that the subordinate will outshine them and tend to be discouraging. Be sensitive to your boss's self-image.

The locomotive and politico want to be viewed as patriarchal. Reinforcement and maintenance of these two bosses' self-interests depend on subordinates respecting their seniority and background. When dealing with such an overbearing boss as the locomotive or a politico who treasures his sacrosanct image (rather than production), we are naturally inclined to turn them off. When this happens often enough, they exaggerate their insipid behavior in an attempt to reestablish themselves. Like a nuclear reactor achieving critical mass, the more the boss presses, the more the subordinate resists until all that's left is a mushroom cloud where your career used to be. Without developing a reputation for apple-polishing, you can make the boss dependent on you for at least partial fulfillment of his self-interest needs.

When the DI feels anxious and out of control, he naturally tries to grasp for more control. Subordinates on whom the DI depends to maintain some semblance of organization can often elude such stringent structure. How many times have you heard a harassed boss applaud the organization of her secretary or assistant? This person keeps the work flowing to and from her boss. Without this key link Hurriup N. Wate, the DI, would be lost. She has become dependent on this associate.

The more a boss relies on you, the more control you are able to exert over your environment. Dependence translates to your effectiveness at firing your boss. There are several techniques to enhance the dependence your boss has on you. These apply to most types of bosses and are easy to exploit with a little thought and application of your talent.

Provide Know-how

If your boss was newly hired or, as in the case of the juvenile boss, was only recently promoted to her position, her inexperience can become your advantage. Chances are that the boss has come into her job short on understanding how to slash through red tape. Additionally, she probably has not become a member of the old boy network yet. With any luck, she never will be, thus making your alliance with this secret society all the more valuable. Understanding how things really get done helps make even the most inept boss appear successful.

Dependence on you can come from each of the following three areas:

- Inside knowledge of accepted methods to get around administrative obstacles;
- Solid working relationships with those who can help your department;
- A sounding board on which the boss can sharpen her managerial skills.

Not only can prudent use of your knowledge of the company and its players help your department, it further enhances the dependence the boss has on you.

Use Your Network of Contacts

Know-how and your network of contacts go hand in hand. If you have been in the company for a while, you have developed friends and allegiances in other departments. Use these contacts to your department's advantage. Call in the markers for past favors. Work your connections within the company to better the department and, vis-à-vis, the boss. When you are successful in doing this, be sure the boss understands who greased the skids.

Manage the Manager

Most subordinates have an intimate knowledge of how their departments could be run more efficiently. Additionally, the pleaser and the juvenile lack many of the skills necessary to lead a group in reaching its goals. Dependence in this area revolves around telling the boss in a straightforward manner just how much supervision the team requires, how much responsibility and authority should be delegated, and how detailed the work instructions need to be. Bosses who are unfamiliar with their positions will appreciate such a helping hand. Others who look upon this as a power struggle will fight it. Such bosses will perceive any suggestion, no matter how helpful, as an assault on their authority. Be cautious and tactful but relentless.

When you propose that you be made responsible for a task, don't frame the proposal as a loss of the boss's authority. This tells the boss that you don't care about his concerns and that you think you know better. Instead, get him to suggest a constructive idea or solution that allows for delegation of authority. The care you demonstrate about your relationship with the boss influences how you feel about your career. Even the most authoritarian locomotives will favor someone who cares enough about themselves to try to help the boss.

Develop a Track Record

Dependence and reliance on subordinates comes from a string of successful campaigns. Bosses with really tough problems will depend more on those who have proved themselves in the past. For a new boss, your track record does not exist because she has not seen it herself. But you can let her know who you are and what you have successfully accomplished under the prior administration.

Let the boss know of your track record. Making sure the boss has seen your résumé might be a good starting point. Additionally, there is nothing wrong with citing successful approaches you have used in the past as possible solutions to a present problem.

When given a chance to add to your successful track record with the boss, don't let him down. A boss faced with a subordinate who just screwed up does not consider the last success. Instead, he asks, "What have you done for me lately?" Consider the projects you are given with care. Assess your ability to complete them successfully within the time YOU have established with your boss. If you see a problem, address it immediately. There is nothing wrong with taking assignments that are challenging. These assignments help you grow professionally. Just make sure you have a safety net so your inexperience doesn't put you and your boss at risk.

Your track record will magnify the boss's dependence when she can forget about a task after she gives it to you, secure in the knowledge that it will be done right.

Loyalty

David Ewing, in his book *Do It My Way or You're Fired* (John Wiley and Sons, New York, NY 1983), cited one executive's philosophy of loyalty: "When it comes to establishing loyalty, I have yet to find a substitute for fear." This intractable old locomotive obviously felt that people cannot be trusted without holding a gun to their heads. Your boss may feel the same way.

Develop an image as someone who values loyalty in himself as much as others. Nobody feels they can trust a turncoat. Lame Duk, the refugee from Peking, works his contacts and sources of information to such a high degree that he can find out if anyone is talking behind his back. Beware of this, and avoid gossip.

If you point the finger at your boss during a conversation with someone else, there are at least three fingers pointing back at you. The person to whom you tell these tales may nod and agree, then wonder what you say about him to other people. If you disagree with the boss or have something to say, say it to his face. People respect members of the loyal opposition more than people with whom they must guess where they stand.

You may not agree with your boss's methods or motives. You both share, however, the same goals for the department or company in which you work. Keep internal problems internal. Solve them without the help of outsiders. As your campaign to fire your boss gathers steam, your work will stand on its own to the people who count in your career. Undermining the boss's position will only slow you down.

The United States has seen a new hierarchy of loyalty values emerge among its young managers. It used to be (and in Japan still remains so to a large extent) that people stayed loyal to their companies throughout their working careers. The company, in return, became responsible for the employee, creating almost a family environment. Increased competition, improved employee job mobility, and the recent epidemic of corporate mergers has caused a shift away from such company-employee relationships. Further, stockholders are not afraid to sue management for "breach of its fiduciary duties." Such a breach often simply means that management failed to make as much money as the disgruntled stockholder thinks it should have.

Employees themselves are being taken to task for not realizing that blind loyalty to a boss can land you in court. The case of Oliver North provides a glimpse into how subordinates can no longer blindly carry out the wishes of their bosses without themselves bearing some responsibility.

If you have a political boss, stay out of his political wars.

Resist the urge to snipe at him or conspire with his enemies. Being a conscientious objector to the boss's political wars may not always be easy. Especially when he drafts you into his army by asking that you write memos lambasting the enemy for some real or imagined offense. Reason your way out. Observe how the boss's relationship with the target has deteriorated since the declaration of war. Remind the boss how the department still needs a working relationship with the target and that one of you should remain untainted.

Become a Confidant

Bosses depend on subordinates with whom they can communicate. If you have developed a strong track record, successfully used your special know-how, and demonstrated a reasonable loyalty, the boss will have no reason not to bring you into his inner circle. Your common sense and informed judgment can be a breath of fresh air to a boss surrounded by unreasonable deadlines, staff gnashing away at his authority, piranhas who gossip behind his back, and the warring factions of his own department for which he sees himself as the lone voice of reason.

Being a trusted confidant means that the boss has faith that he can tell you anything and it will not be used against him nor will he hear it in the halls afterward. Additionally, the boss knows that your conclusions are supported by research, tempered with the judgment borne from experience, and that you have no objective other than providing the right answer to the problem. Your boss will depend much more on the judgment of a subordinate who does not allow the boss's opinion to influence his thinking. Finally, the boss must have confidence that you will not turn against him when the going gets tough. These qualities make for a good confidant.

Make Decisions

Don't shy away from decisions. Dependence on you for this vital action comes once the boss trusts your judgment and experience. The political boss often doesn't mind having his subordinates take on some of this responsibility. He can disavow knowledge of their actions should something go wrong. The DI needs to have someone make decisions when he comes down with an all-too-frequent case of analysis paralysis.

I once heard a story of a locomotive publishing executive we'll call the Orient Express. Express found it necessary to approve every manuscript her editors purchased. Everyone knew she had a pet peeve against accepting a particular category of book for publication. One of her editors waited until she was on vacation, then accepted just such a book on his own authority. When the locomotive steamed back from vacation, she was livid at what her subordinate had done. There was nothing she could do to cancel the deal. Later, the book became a runaway best-seller. Express has not questioned the editor's judgment since.

Consolidation of your power base comes when you take over responsibility for decisions in a particular area. The boss comes to depend on you for your remarkable abilities in that area. From there you are free to expand the base outward to other aspects of your job.

MAKE THE BOSS COMFORTABLE BEING DEPENDENT

With dependence comes a measure of power over the boss. Smart bosses are on the lookout to verify that their trust was well-founded. As the boss becomes more comfortable with his reliance on you, he will relinquish more of the things you need to operate without his interference. Here are some tools you can use to heighten the boss's level of comfort:

Feedback

When the boss lets go some of her authority, keep her informed of the decisions you have made and your reasoning behind them. When the results are in, let the boss know how it went. As your string of successes grows, so does the boss's confidence that the authority, which she formerly had, is in good hands.

Trust

Trust engenders comfort. Give the boss reason to trust you. Let the boss know that you are a responsible person who will not abuse the authority with which you have been entrusted.

Mistakes

Never try to cover up a mistake or blame it on circumstances beyond your control. There should be very little beyond your control (with respect to your job), anyway. If you have earned the boss's trust and you blow it, take complete responsibility. The boss must be confident that tasks given to you are yours completely, whether they succeed or fail.

The Team Concept

Bosses are most comfortable with subordinates whose motivations are consistent with their own. Success of the department and its goals should be one of your motivating factors. Your career will prosper as long as you make sure that you have played an integral role in the team's success.

Standards of Excellence

A reputation as a perfectionist will do you little harm as long as you don't let it get in the way of achieving the objective. The boss must be familiar with your standards and agree that they indeed match his own.

Communicate Effectively

Your boss must be able to understand the signals you give her. Make your presentations as concise as possible. The most effective communications are in summary form. The entire idea should be described in no more than a few sentences. Let the boss ask for greater detail if necessary. There are few things more exasperating than someone who doesn't really know what he wants to say but makes his audience sit through a lengthy history of the world in the hope that somewhere in there exists the thought he wanted to convey.

Personality

You are definitely not in a popularity contest. Yet neither are you out to win "ogre of the year." All of us are most comfortable with convivial personalities. You should not be a yes-person, nor should you argue just because you want to be assertive. When you must be contrary, choose your venues carefully. When you stand up for your opinion, do so without wavering. Argue your case as an adult—calmly and forcefully. Don't get mad. Keep the discussion from becoming personal.

DOS AND DON'TS OF DEPENDENCE

Dependent bosses must be finely tuned. Too much dependence and you become so valuable that promotion may have to wait until you can be replaced. Not enough dependence and you loose the leverage over your boss that this valuable quality can deliver. To help you achieve the right balance, follow this list of Dos and Don'ts.

DOS AND DON'TS OF DEPENDENCE

Dos	*Don'ts*
1. Identify your boss type. Techniques which work for one do not always work for others.	1. Never withhold information from the boss (especially the politico).
2. Point out prior successes of your judgment.	2. Never allow the boss to think you have usurped his authority.
3. Always have a successor to take your place should a promotion come up.	3. Don't become a "yes man."
4. Protect your own turf.	4. Never let others make your decisions for you.
5. Use your authority judiciously.	5. Do not abuse your power.

6. Make sure the information you pass on is accurate.
7. Work for the good of the team.
8. Keep your mouth shut unless:
   a) You can say something good.
   b) You can contribute to the discussion.

6. Do not pass on gossip or allude to innuendo.
7. Never try to intimidate your boss.
8. Never bad-mouth the competition. This only starts wars.

9. Resist stating the obvious.
10. Do not allow your boss to depend on you for use as a whipping boy.

VI

Two for the Show: Demanding Authority and Conquering Your Boss

"Ken, you backstabbing swine. As my cash manager, you are supposed to make sure the bank account has enough money to clear the checks we write. The bank president just called to tell me that we're $150,000 overdrawn. He had the nerve to ask if I knew what went on in my own shop."

Bristling with the unfairness of this new accusation, Ken finally explodes, "Listen, asshole, you refused to give me check-signing authority. You refused to allow me to make telephone wire transfers. Besides, you were out playing golf when I needed to move the money, and you forgot to sign the authorization. How can I do my job when I don't have the necessary tools?"

Responsibility and authority go hand in hand. Maladroit bosses like the juvenile, Princess Rising Star, and I. B. Meantuu, the locomotive, retain authority as a sign of their control, their stature, and their importance. Responsibility without authority to act parallels the injustice of taxation without representation and will leave you powerless. Lack of authority places you at the mercy of an unskilled and possibly incompetent boss. In short, authority is the highest compliment you can receive—even more so if your authority is awarded by removing it from someone else, like your boss.

Responsibility for a task ideally should carry with it complete authority to execute the job from start to finish. In my travels I once came across a small company whose sales manager had the responsibility of supervising five salespeople. The sales manager's boss, the vice president of sales, retained the authority to hire, fire, promote, and give raises as well as performance reviews. The salespeople still perceived the vice president as their immediate boss. The sales manager had no authority and could not implement any of his plans and objectives. He allowed himself to be saddled by responsibility without authority and ultimately failed.

Unfortunately with most bosses authority becomes a symbol of power. I. B. Meantuu, the locomotive, withholds authority out of fear that subordinates will gain too much power and no longer need him. Harriup N. Wate, the DI, shilly-shallies away from granting authority out of a conviction (some say it's inbred in the DI genes) that no one can do the job as well as she. Princess Rising Star, the juvenile, simply has not yet learned how to manage and when to delegate authority. Lame Duk, being the consummate politician, has a black belt in delegating responsibility (to set up a perfect scapegoat) without transferring the power, which would weaken his political base.

The example at the beginning of this chapter of Ken the cash manager illustrates classic responsibility without authority at the hands of a political boss. Ken's self-destructive mistakes made him a convenient goat just asking to be used. First, Ken's boss probably had a history of not delegating authority to his people yet held them responsible for particular tasks. Ken allowed this damaging practice to perpetuate itself. Second, the boss obviously was unavailable at key times. Ken should have insisted that the boss grant specific authority (check-signing and telephone-transfer authority). This should not have been too difficult because there was an obvious need and it would have made the boss more mobile (something politicians need when out on junkets). Failing to secure the authority to do his job, Ken should have foreseen certain failure and confronted his boss while his good reputation was still intact. Because Ken failed to halt his incompetent boss from continuing this dangerous practice, resignation or transfer to a different department would have placed him in a stronger position than having to leave under a cloud as he now must consider.

INTERACTION OF AUTHORITY AND RESPONSIBILITY

Most of us use authority to execute our responsibilities. Few sensible people would consider taking on the responsibility for piloting an airplane without the authority to land whenever, wherever, and for whatever reason we felt necessary to ensure the safety of their passengers. The responsibility you take for your career and your job requires that type of authority. Without it, you place yourself at the mercy of someone lacking your familiarity with the special issues and goals associated with your career.

Authority and responsibility complement each other. People who have authority want to use it. When they use their authority, they usually become responsible for the outcome. People who duck responsibility for actions they authorize don't last very long in positions of power. How would you feel about Tip Blabbermeister whom you gave the responsibility and authority to install emergency lighting at the hospital you run? Two days after it was installed Tip's lighting did not work during a storm. His excuse was that the chief engineer did not test it after installation. You would first want to wire Tip to the system, then test it yourself.

LEVELS OF RESPONSIBILITY AND AUTHORITY

When you fire your boss, you take responsibility for your own career. At the same time, you remove the authority formerly held by your boss to help guide your career. This becomes a matter of attitude more than anything else. To preserve their authority to make career decisions for employees (which first and foremost are for the good of themselves), many bosses fantasize that they know what's good for their people. Don't swallow this bilge. Your boss does not have your best interests at heart; she advances first her own concerns, then whatever twisted obligation she perceives she owes to the company. When Letsall Getalong asks again, "Don't you trust me?" the answer is still an emphatic NO!

The order of priorities perceived by today's young managers has been shifting over time. It used to be that responsibility to the employer ranked near the top. This has changed to something comparable to the following hierarchy:

RESPONSIBILITY HIERARCHY OF THE NINETIES

First: Responsibility for oneself and family needs;
Second: Responsibility to your profession (i.e., you can easily get another job, you can't easily change professions);
Third: Responsibility for your subordinates and to your co-workers;

Fourth: Responsibility to the company;
Fifth: Responsibility to the boss.

First Level of Responsibility

Your first level of responsibility and authority to act on behalf of your own career comes from and is for the good of yourself and your family. Failure to meet your full potential and career aspirations can be blamed on bad luck, poor timing, and incompetent bosses. These, however, are only excuses. You must ultimately shoulder the responsibility and you alone have absolute authority to act on your own behalf.

Second Level of Responsibility

The second level of responsibility goes to your profession. You can always get another job, but few people successfully change professions without first taking several steps backward. Many professions consider the responsibilities and authority to uphold professional ideals so important that they have standards of conduct that their members are required to abide by. This is true of the public accounting, legal, and medical professions, to name a few.

Bosses who ask a subordinate to behave in a manner inconsistent with the standards of conduct promulgated by the subordinate's profession are obviously placing themselves and their own needs ahead of the employee's. Such bosses cannot be respected and must be fired for your own professional good. The subordinate has a responsibility to her profession (as well as the authority that has been upheld by many labor boards) to refuse to perform in a manner that conflicts with the profession's rules of conduct.

Third Level of Responsibility

The third level of responsibility and authority goes to your subordinates and co-workers. These people depend on you for guidance and leadership. Only by their consent are you allowed to lead. It bears repeating that every time you open your mouth or make a decision you either fortify or weaken that authority. As you develop a track record of successes with your people, their trust in your abilities will increase. With such trust, they gradually will allow you more and more latitude as their boss. Unlike Letsall Getalong, a good leader does not have to ask, "Don't you trust me?" The answer has been given many times over in many situations in which the leader has proved his resourcefulness.

Fourth Level of Responsibility

The fourth level of responsibility and authority derives from the company that employs you. Don't confuse your employer with your boss. The company that employs you will survive long after your incompetent boss bites the dust.

Your company entrusts its employees to do their jobs to their best abilities. The company provides management to direct the employees in their work and furnishes resources to allow the work to be done. In return, the company gives its employees the responsibility and authority to act on its behalf for its betterment. If you need additional responsibility and authority to execute your job and your boss does not see it that way, your higher obligation is to the company. In these enlightened times, there is room for professional disagreement between boss and subordinate. You owe your employer the benefit of your knowledge. Further, it is your responsibility to make yourself heard.

Your authority to go over your boss's head comes from your obligation to the company.

Basement Level of Responsibility

The final level in the responsibility/authority hierarchy ends with the boss. Because he's last does not make this obligation and responsibility unimportant. On the contrary, your boss must be dealt with on a daily basis. He provides you the most direct feedback and can help or hinder your career goals more than any single person other than yourself. Your responsibility to the boss begins with doing your job to the best of your ability. It extends far beyond that, however. You must also keep him informed of what assistance you need to more successfully execute your job. You must direct him in his supervisory duties toward you. You owe him a certain amount of loyalty. Whatever influence he has over you, which impacts your ability to do your job, you are responsible to ensure its adequacy. Where your boss hinders rather than helps you do your job, you are obligated to correct him.

The authority you derive to execute this responsibility comes from both yourself (in managing your own career and success) and from the employer who pays you. Bosses who are inadequate must be fired from your career for your own good as well as that of your employer. This is your responsibility.

RESPONSIBILITY AND AUTHORITY AS RELATED TO YOUR JOB

Some people fear success as much as they do failure. With success comes the unknown. People may ask, What will she want me to do now after I've become the inventory maven?

On-the-Job Responsibility

Doing your job well means accepting responsibility. Once you have accepted responsibilities and incorporated them into your daily job routine, the supervisory burden on your boss will be diminished. Securing the majority of supervisory responsibilities and authority goes a long way toward achieving independence from an incompetent boss. The four key elements of on-the-job responsibility include the following:

Timeliness

In business, as with most things in life, timing is everything. Differences between success and failure are often determined by the timing of performance. The most basic element of timing responsibility deals with your presence on the job when you are needed. When you fire your boss and take on most supervisory responsibilities yourself, you are obligated to place yourself in the position where you can best contribute to the company's success whenever and wherever necessary. By now it should be clear that when you fire your boss, you are no longer a nine-to-five employee. If you think you could get more of your job done by coming in early or by leaving a little later, do it.

The next, more tricky part of this first element of on-the-job responsibility has to do with coordinating the timing of your job into that of the rest of the company. This task used to be done by your supervisor before you fired him. Now you must be sensitive as to the timing of key elements of your job and how they relate to the overall effort. For example, if your job includes engineering a new alloy for use on the airframe of a prototype airplane, your on-the-job responsibility necessitates coordinating with the structural engineering department to find out when they need certain answers from you.

Accuracy

The second element of on-the-job responsibility deals with reliance on the accuracy of your work. The DI, Imagonna Grabontoitz, takes great pleasure in dressing down his subordinates for sloppy or inaccurate work. He uses this to conceal his disorganization and outright incompetence. As your own boss, now you must take over the task of review and revision of your work. This may be one of the more difficult things you do.

Few things rival the boredom of reading a report you wrote and checking for errors, inconsistency of logic, redundancy, and faulty thinking. Everyone tends to become slack when reviewing their own work. Question your basic premises, try to explain to a layperson how and why you arrived at your conclusions and decisions. Become your own most vigorous critic. When your work passes your review, give it to someone whose judgment you value and trust. Invite that person to tear it apart. Only when you are satisfied that your work product reflects an accuracy you are proud of should it be submitted to your boss.

Feedback

Once you have fired your boss from your career, you are no longer a blind servant of the boss's commands. You have taken responsibility for evaluating and changing, when necessary, the boss's dicta. One of the reasons most people feel the need to fire their boss stems from a lack of confidence in the boss's leadership ability. Such mistrust originates from reservations about the boss's judgment, priorities, and motivations. Responsibility to your career and your employer requires you to exercise your own judgment when interpreting the boss's instructions, evaluating her goals, and assessing her description of what the finished product will look like.

When these things are inconsistent, you must bring them first to the boss's attention for an explanation. If you receive no satisfaction regarding your reservations, you are obligated to seek someone else with authority to correct what you see as a problem.

After the tragedy of the space shuttle *Challenger*, NASA instituted a vigorous program of objective feedback and evaluation for each phase of the launch procedure. Instead of certifying that each major system was ready for flight, the agency now goes on the presumption that the system IS NOT airworthy. It then becomes the job of the managers to prove to the launch director that the system will perform properly.

Creativity and Judgment

The reason you fired your boss stems in part from your refusal to have your own creativity and judgment ignored. I. B. Meantuu, the locomotive, probably has indeed forgotten more about widgets than you know right now. Nevertheless, that does not give him the right to stifle your professional growth while traipsing over your career. Firing your boss means that you have now taken responsibility for using your creativity and judgment to do your own job better. No longer can you accept Meantuu's dictum that his way is the only way. You are obligated to use your skills to execute your job.

Authority to Do Your Job

Locomotives like Meantuu, DIs like Grabontoitz, and juveniles like Her Royal Highness Rising Star are reluctant to surrender their authority. These bosses are infamous, however, for taking their subordinates to task if they fail in their responsibilities. Neglecting to obtain proper authority provides no excuse. After all, when you fired your inept boss, whose job was it to convince him that you needed proper authority to do your job?

Meantuu, Grabontoitz, and Star can be persuaded to at least share their authority if they are shown a business reason that doesn't threaten their perceived superiority and if it provides a better product for which they can share credit. A project that is delayed because the subordinate had to wait for her boss to return to sign equipment orders provides a case in point.

These three bosses are convinced that the company will fall apart if they are not physically present. But everyone must leave the office sometime. Absence provides a perfect opportunity to have the boss grant temporary authority, which would have otherwise been difficult to pry loose. When the boss returns and sees that everything went smoothly because he trusted you, a case can be made for keeping the authority, which had originally been granted only temporarily. You have gotten the boss used to trusting you.

Bosses who use their authority and delegate it properly can compound their effectiveness. But Letsall Getalong, the pleaser, tends to confuse subordinates when delegating authority by being vague as to exactly how much authority has been extended and under what circumstances it may be exercised. Politicians like Lyan Lobby purposely create an "authority gap" by delegating limited authority to subordinates. Such a gap places Lobby squarely between the limited power delegated and the power required to complete the job. He still retains control while maintaining the illusion of being a good delegator. Typical of the Lyan Lobby we've come to know, don't you think? Perhaps even typical of your own boss.

Types of Authority

There are many authorities which are applied on a formal and informal basis every business day. Wise use of authority makes the company run smoothly. Authority imprudently applied throws sand into the machinery of a formerly well oiled enterprise.

The first authority which you must have to execute your responsibilities includes the ability to obtain whatever resources are required to do your job. The reasoning behind this authorization includes your familiarity with the daily job requirements and your ability to expedite needed resources on a more basic level than the boss. Additionally, resources often cannot be bought "off the rack"—that is, there are specifications that must be translated and interpreted. By going through various levels of management, the risk of error increases while the time required stretches out. Signature authority to obtain supplies goes a long way toward separating your boss's powers from yours. Additionally, your status gets elevated.

You must have decision-making authority to become your own boss. The locomotive in particular guards this ego enhancer as if it were the gold in Fort Knox. By binding I. B. Meantuu's large ego to his ability as a teacher you can take over the decision making as if it were a learning experience. As Meantuu becomes more comfortable in his new role as a developer of people, the decision-making authority becomes yours. Politicians like Tip Blabbermeister will hand over the keys to the city if they view it as politically expedient. Delegation of decision-making authority and responsibility limits Tip's risk factor.

The authority to cross departmental lines when necessary can be handy and conveys significant power and trust in you. Politicians like Lame Duk want the spotlight on themselves. Duk would rather have you just stay inside the district and not venture into the arena where he has proclaimed himself the master. Princess Rising Star, on the other hand, wants to stick her nose into everything both in and outside of her department. The authority to cut across departmental lines usually resides with Her Royal Highness unless a coup is mounted. Not only will having authorization to interact with other departments improve your work product, it will also fulfill an important requirement of leadership: understanding and controlling how your role fits into the entire scheme of things. Additionally, your abilities will be displayed to others in the company who can help your career. Dependence on an unqualified boss becomes lessened.

Many bosses proclaim an open-door policy. If your boss's boss has this policy be careful how you use it. In reality this policy usually exists only in the boss's mind. Subordinates who take advantage of this policy are usually berated by their immediate bosses for going over their heads. Such a subordinate becomes particularly dangerous for Lyan Lobby who finds it essential to control the spin of information going out of his department. However, when the boss's boss feels you have something to say and invites you to speak freely whenever you wish, your status and importance skyrockets.

Spokesperson authority parallels the power to go directly to the boss's boss and the ability to cross departmental lines. Even though you may only be the spokesperson for your own job, at least you get to do the talking. Such authority allows you the chance to present your case honestly and completely without any self-serving double-talk from a boss trying to protect himself. Additionally, it bestows on you a certain amount of expertise and trust. Independence from an incapable boss can be enhanced by obtaining the authority to speak for yourself or for him (though probably only in his absence).

Many large companies have a formal transfer of authority routine. When a key individual will be unavailable, some of her powers are formally transferred to someone else. This can be particularly important with signature authorities, which must be on file at such places as banks and government offices. Other authorities are less formal but no less important. When your boss does transfer specific authorities to you, try to get it in writing if possible. This leaves no doubt in anyone's mind as to what has taken place, and it can be shown to those who may require proof that you are indeed authorized to act.

Authority + Responsibility = Independence

Once you have accepted responsibility for your job and have a series of successes that prove it, you will have a strong case for demanding the authority needed to act independently. With responsibility and authority, you have the most important ingredients needed to free yourself of an incompetent boss.

Use your new independence sensibly. Locomotives like I. B. Meantuu and DIs like Imagonna Grabontoitz are overworked because they allow themselves to be. Their subordinates are underchallenged by bosses who insist on assembly line routine. These types of bosses are often found in large organizations where authority has been given to Meantuu or Grabontoitz more to ensure that established rules are followed rather than to make meaningful decisions. Both Meantuu and Grabontoitz treat subordinates as mere expediters of their orders. Now that you have distanced yourself from the ill effects of that type of boss, learn from their bad example. If you treat your subordinates similarly, the authority they have conferred on you to be their manager will soon be snatched back.

As a string of successes develops, your opinion will be given greater weight. Use this to cement your independence, making it impossible to lapse back into your former relationship with your boss. Do this by never forgetting whom you work for: yourself. Remember your four areas of on-the-job responsibility, and don't disappoint those who depend on you.

SELL AUTHORITY AND RESPONSIBILITY TO THE BOSS

Few bosses willingly relinquish their authority and what they understand to be their responsibilities to a subordinate. Many things go into release of authority such as ego, earning the right to authority by having paid one's dues, trust in your judgment, perception by the boss's boss—the list goes on. They must be sold, and you are just the one to do it. Here's how.

Step 1: Gain the Boss's Confidence

Not even the most irresponsible DI will transfer responsibility to someone who she does not believe can do the job. Gain the boss's trust by paying attention to the details of your job. It makes no sense to do a terrific job painting the fence only to find that the color should have been white instead of red.

You've undoubtedly heard bosses like the DI, Hurriup N. Wate, proclaim themselves to paint with a broad brush and that only they see the big picture. What success they may have had in their careers, however, was probably based on a series of baby steps, each concerned with the details on which a project stands or falls. Gain the boss's confidence that you are detail oriented and will not let things fall through the cracks.

Step 2: Demonstrate Ability

Your record of achievement establishes your ability. Part of any sales presentation contains a list of satisfied customers. Remind the boss of those times where you had to take command of the situation, assumed authority, and succeeded in doing what needed to be done. If the particular situation you are after is a little different, tell the boss how you will handle those differences. Finally, recall the unique parts of your background (degrees, courses, seminars, and practical experience) that have prepared you to do what you are asking.

Step 3: When All Else Fails, Use Logic

Logic has its place in most sales presentations. It becomes most effective, however, when employed as a building block that supports the emotional reasons with which the boss will agree. Logic for receiving responsibility and the authority to execute your job includes:

- You are closer to the situation than your boss.
- You have a minute-by-minute understanding of the problems and solutions that come up every day.
- You can act faster without the burden of having to go through the review-and-approval process created by an extra layer of management.
- Without having someone to pass the baton, the boss cannot move up (succession).

Step 4: Contingency Plans

Deal with the boss's objections before he mentions them. Locomotives in particular like to bring up "what if" questions (What will you do if . . . , How would you handle . . . , Have you thought of . . .). This seems to secure their perception of being needed. Don't claim to have all the answers, but insist that you know how to get help if necessary. Leaders have confidence that they can untangle themselves from most any scrape they get into. If possible, cite past instances where you had to reason your way out of a problem situation and you did just fine.

Step 5: Saving Face

I. B. Meantuu, the locomotive, has much of his ego wrapped up in the job. You are dead if he perceives that you want to strip him of his hard-fought status. Your presentation should not be adversarial (e.g., I win, you lose). Instead, make him understand how much more good he can accomplish by delegating some of his responsibilities and authority to a subordinate whom he himself has taught. All the better if Meantuu views delegating authority as his own idea.

To Tip Blabbermeister image is everything. Your sales presentation should be one where his image can be enhanced by delegating certain responsibilities and authorities to you. Further, the argument of succession can be reinforced. Watch for signs, however, that Tip will grant limited authority in order to create the authority gap described earlier. Limited authority means no authority at all because you are still dependent on the boss.

Princess Rising Star, the juvenile, and Letsall Getalong, the pleaser, can be dealt with more bluntly. If they have given you responsibilities without the necessary authority to do an effective job, you will certainly fail. Suggest that you may relinquish the responsibilities in question entirely rather than allow the blemish of failure on your record. In our up-or-out corporate society, word will certainly get out as to the management style that prompted a promising employee to refuse responsibility rather than face an almost certain failure. Few superstars such as Star are willing to risk a public admission of having failed in their managerial obligations.

Step 6: Benefits

Your boss will wonder why he did not delegate sooner once he sees the amount of extra time he has for those who really need his help. When word gets out how the boss develops his people and gives them their own lead, there will be a stampede of bright young people wanting to learn from the master. Better decisions made faster and with less likelihood of error will produce a better product.

The benefits of participative management are legion. It all starts with giving you the responsibility and authority to do your job completely without unnecessary help from the boss.

Step 7: Close the Sale

You've come a long way. All the effort you've expended in gaining the boss's confidence, demonstrating your ability, making a logical case for what you want, dealing with the boss's objections, allowing him to save face and to see the benefits get summarized in the close. Different people use a variety of closes depending on the situation and who's buying.

Try simply asking if there is anything the boss can think of that would prohibit him from giving you the responsibility and authority you've asked for. Don't take a "maybe" as an answer. Lyan Lobby, in the great political tradition, may say that you make a good case but he needs time to study it. Ask what reservations he has, then deal with them on the spot. Try closing again. Do not let the boss slither away without giving you a commitment.

TECHNIQUES OF SEIZING AUTHORITY AND RESPONSIBILITY

Strong men and women have strong weaknesses. Tough bosses will try every trick to retain their responsibilities and authority. There are, however, some things you can do to whittle away that crusty exterior:

1. Begin making decisions for the boss subject to his approval. Soon he'll begin to respect your judgment, and he'll give you formal authorization.
2. Make sure people know you as a person, not as an unthinking functionary who merely does the boss's bidding.
3. Be sure that your work gets the attention it deserves. For example, don't let the boss dismiss a report you wrote by saying, "Lay it on my desk; I'll read it later." Respond with, "I'll just keep it until we can discuss it. Would tomorrow at nine be OK?"
4. Develop a support network apart from the boss. These partisans can help persuade obdurate bosses to give you a chance. Additionally, they can help should you get in over your head.

DOS AND DON'TS FOR AUTHORITY AND RESPONSIBILITY

Dos	*Don'ts*
1. Direct boss to make strategic decisions. You should make tactical decisions.	1. Never allow the boss to delegate accountability. That's what he is paid for.

---

2. Clarify the rules at the beginning in terms of:
   a) what authority has been delegated
   b) when that authority can be used
   c) exact definition of the work product
   d) timing of completion

2. Resist trying to eliminate the boss's job. Just be sure it does not interfere with yours.

3. Specify the boss's role in terms of:
   a) supervision
   b) accountability
   c) responsibility
   d) authority

3. Don't allow the boss to provide an incomplete overview of the task and its purpose. Insist on knowing everything YOU think is relevant regardless of what your boss says.

4. Establish milestones with goals and timing specified.

4. Don't allow authority gaps where the boss tries to retain control.

5. Demand complete authority to get the job done without resorting to the boss's authority.

6. Monitor performance signals from other parts of the company.

5. Don't commit to unrealistic timing goals. Be sure timing includes space for periodic reports to the boss, inclusion of her input, and mid-course corrections.

VII

Three to Get Ready: Beg, Borrow, or Steal, But Get Resources

"Ted, I heard a lot of commotion in your shop yesterday after the power failed and everyone went home. Anything wrong?"

Ted explained to the company president that his group continued their work using lights driven by the power from three portable electric generators he rented that day. The president had not been aware that there would be a $10,000 penalty if Ted's group's circuit boards were not shipped yesterday. Ted spent $700 on generators to light the area for seven hours so that the boards could be packed and shipped. The president scratched his head and wondered if he would have thought of that. He would later remember both Ted's initiative at saving a net $9,300 in penalties and why Ted's boss, who was paid to think of such things, didn't.

Business does not measure performance in terms of how hard you tried or how long you worked. Business measures performance in terms of success. Did you deliver? Period. Excuses, while they may be valid, are seldom passed up the corporate ladder because they tend to reflect negatively downward. To a large extent, success depends on your ability to marshal the resources that are necessary to get the job done. Because resources are scarce at most companies, you must compete against other equally pressing demands to obtain what you need to succeed. Dependence on a boss without the clout necessary to obtain the resources her people need to do their jobs makes failures of us all. When you fire your boss, the luxury of having someone provide scarce resources no longer exists. You must obtain them yourself.

There are three channels that supply scarce resources:

- Those that are generally accepted and proper;
- The so-called back channel—less formal but often provides quick resources;
- Channels that use guerrilla warfare tactics.

Establishing reliable resource channels and knowing when to use them will assure you of having the things required to do your job. They will also further increase the power and independence you exercise over your boss.

RESOURCES AND YOUR BOSS

Different boss types cause various kinds of resource problems. Experience, connections, and motivations trigger the boss's access to and allocation of resources.

I. B. Meantuu, the locomotive, has so much experience that he knows which resources are important and which are not. He doesn't waste time seeking the things that might eventually be useful but concentrates instead on exactly what will get him where he wants to go. Further, because of his tenure, he has constructed a back channel that has become so routine that it has all but replaced normal resource pipelines.

Politicians like Tip Blabbermeister use resources as a support for their power base. Just as favors can be traded back and forth in the political arena, so can resources. In fact, underground economies spring up in some organizations where company resources are bartered among managers and between divisions. This is particularly true of the military where good relationships with supply sergeants can be invaluable. Amassing coveted corporate resources can greatly enhance the clout a politician wields. Equally important are past favors owed by others, which can be converted to resources as needed. When you fire Blabbermeister, make sure that you have access to some or all of the resources that he controls.

Letsall Getalong, the pleaser, too frequently gives up needed resources in the hope of generating goodwill. This may be one of the reasons why you found it necessary to terminate his influence over your career in the first place. Getalong's subordinates often have to make do with old, worn-out equipment, scrimpy budgets, and insufficient help because their boss was too weak to speak up. This hits home when bonuses are allocated among departments and Letsall, once again, caves in by allowing someone else to take a portion of his allocation.

Our resident DIs, Imagonna Grabontoitz and Hurriup N. Wate, have yet to figure out what resources are important. They each have a hard time allocating resources to get maximum utility. Because of his disorganization and penchant for fire fighting, Grabontoitz very well may throw them at whatever problem threatens the most damage at the moment. His knee-jerk reactions occur without regard to efficiency or adequacy. Hurriup N. Wate, on the other hand, often fails to recognize just what resources her subordinates need to do their jobs. She often accepts tools that are inappropriate for the job at hand or that can be made to work only after much additional effort and frustration.

Princess Rising Star, being a juvenile boss, has not been around long enough yet to establish a back channel for resource supply. She relies almost exclusively on formal asset-allocation procedures and guerrilla warfare. Her skills, however, at guerrilla tactics need development. Consequently, she makes enemies right off the bat, appears domineering and numbed to the overall objectives of the company.

RESOURCES NECESSARY TO DO YOUR JOB

The things you need in order to do your job accurately and on time constitute resources. Most desirable resources are in short supply. Some incompetent bosses snag the scarcest of resources and salt them away for later use, thus keeping them from those who could use them now. The key to independence from an inept boss lies in control over your own resources. Some common resources that you must obtain include the following:

People

People resources are the most expensive, the most difficult to manage, and in the most limited supply. The more technically demanding your job, the fewer people you will have available to assist you. Locomotives like I. B. Meantuu fail to recognize that managers are paid to manage, not to do the work themselves. To them, nobody is as good as they are, therefore, everyone is expendable. On the contrary, as your own boss you will quickly learn that the way you treat your subordinates dictates output, creativity, and your ability to recruit more qualified people.

Enough of the right people assigned to the wrong jobs can sink you just as quickly as a dearth of unqualified subordinates can. Don't be afraid to reassign people to jobs they would be better suited for. You need to get the group moving toward a common goal. That can be done only by maximizing the skills of everyone. Critically assess the contribution made by each person. Clear any deadwood away rather than let its rot spread to the rest of the group.

I was once part of a new management team sent in to run a company acquired by a large bank. When I got there, I found many personnel problems caused by a faulty promotion policy. In fact, when we rated the performance of the staff compared with their salaries, we found the highest paid people were often the poorest-rated performers. The staff had known about this for some time but were never consulted by management. The problem had caused a very high attrition rate and had created a demotivating work atmosphere. We completely reshuffled the jobs in the firm. People who were unqualified for their jobs were either moved to more appropriate positions or were fired. There were also several promotions for people who deserved them.

This caused much discomfort for those who were not toeing the line. It also disrupted the work flow for a time, because many qualified people who were never allowed to make decisions before were now in positions of authority. Yet within three months turnover was down, salary expenses were down, productivity was up, and we had developed an atmosphere that rewarded excellence.

People resources are among the most important assets of any company. Be certain you have enough of the right people and deploy them where they will do the most good.

Expertise

Some of the people in your group arrive with enough expertise to make an immediate contribution. Others must be nurtured with patience and education, and then be allowed time to blossom.

As your own boss, you must locate people with the expertise you may lack. In most technical disciplines, the body of knowledge changes so rapidly that all the expertise needed will seldom be found within your own department. You must locate reliable skill resources, which can be tapped when you need them. Such reservoirs of knowledge include your colleagues in other departments or even competitor firms. They can be found in the ranks of retired employees from your own company. Consulting firms provide specialized skills on an as needed basis.

It has been my pleasure to observe Heather, the young chief financial officer (CFO) of a rapidly growing company, mature into her job. Heather had little accounting background when she was asked to become her company's CFO. She did, however, enjoy the complete trust of management and was well liked by everyone. In the areas where she lacked the financial expertise to deal with issues confronting her, she quickly formed a cadre of knowledgeable people from whom she could draw the information she needed. This "brain pool" included her independent CPA firm, my consulting firm, her law firm, and several CFOs from outside firms. Because of her engaging personality, her capacity to grasp concepts quickly, and her fearless ability to admit she didn't know an answer, most of us in her kitchen cabinet never even charged when she called with routine questions. Her career has grown with her company and has greatly contributed to its success.

As your own boss, you cannot afford to falter due to lack of expertise. Not knowing how to solve a particular problem lends little excuse. You are paid to either flatten barricades yourself or find someone who can do it for you. Either way, the responsibility rests with you.

Equipment

Enough of the right equipment can make the difference between meeting a deadline and blowing it. Your ability to command equipment resources reflects directly on your ability as your own boss. Both Letsall Getalong, the pleaser, and the juvenile Rising Star have problems in the equipment area. Getalong's resolve withers when competing for equipment against the likes of politicians such as Lyan Lobby. Star simply doesn't have the mettle to prevent Meantuu from barreling right over her with his seniority and seemingly infinite knowledge about what the company needs and his ability to provide it.

I once knew of a financial printing firm that was very dependent on computers for typesetting and managing print runs. The plant manager unsuccessfully fought for the purchase of a small backup computer to be used in the event something happened to the primary system. Unfortunately, he lost his argument to the company's locomotive president who claimed that the modern primary computer was very reliable. The president was right, the computer was very reliable. What he failed to consider, however, was that it needed electricity to run. One day the power went out for a period of ten hours.

The plant manager had felt so strongly about the need for a backup that he had long ago arranged access to another computer located in a city thirty miles away in event of an emergency. By the time power was restored, the backup computer had completed its typesetting job and the presses rolled with little disruption.

Equipment requirements change frequently. In the example at the beginning of this chapter, no one knew that portable electric generators would save the day. The company did not even have them in its warehouse. Yet Ted's ability to secure them demonstrated his capacity to act decisively and without assistance from the boss whom he fired from his career.

Rules regarding equipment resources can be summarized as:

1. Anticipate equipment requirements.
2. Construct reliable conduits to secure needed equipment.
3. Train people to use equipment to its best and most efficient advantage.
4. Where equipment breakdowns can cause you to fail in your mission, reduce the risk by having an appropriate (not excessive and not clandestine) backup supply.
5. Keep your equipment in a serviceable state. If it is broken, fix it. If it is worn out, replace it.
6. Have people on staff who are adept at fixing equipment resources.

Funding

Adequate funding and budget allocations constitute major resources. People grade a person's importance based in part on the amount of budgeted funds allocated to the task. Without sufficient money to spend, you must always rely on others to provide the resources that enable you to do your job. Such dependence creates an obligation on your part. Be aware that you are expected to return favors, and they may be called in at inopportune times.

Facilities

For some types of tasks, facilities constitute a significant resource. Both politicians like Lame Duk and juveniles like Rising Star consider facilities a statement on their importance. Imagonna Grabontoitz, the DI, however, appears oblivious to his surroundings—probably because he's too busy trying to battle the fires he started.

Apart from prestige, consider the facility in which you work. If it impedes progress, get it changed if possible. In areas where real estate values have substantially appreciated, it could make sense to sell your old facility and lease something more appropriate. Profit from this transaction can be computed by subtracting the sale price of the old facility from the net present value of the lease obligation for new quarters plus interest income from investment of the sale proceeds. This goes to the company's coffers with a considerable dose of distinction thrown your way.

People do not enjoy working in substandard facilities. If your job requires you to recruit outstanding individuals, this will become increasingly difficult the more dilapidated your quarters become. This does not mean that you require a palace. Rather, you should have adequate facilities to do the job and not detract from your effort.

Information

Tip Blabbermeister appreciates the value of information resources. He thinks of them, however, in terms of the infamous "Deep Throat" of Watergate renown. Politicians such as Tip consider information a commodity that can be traded for personal gain. Juveniles such as Princess Rising Star have yet to develop an effective information network. Probably the most effective users of information are locomotives such as I. B. Meantuu. They have been around so long that they probably founded the old boy network in your company.

The more information you have, the greater your ability to seize opportunities for your group and to short-circuit problems before they explode into catastrophes. As your own boss, you need to know where to get necessary information and how to assess its importance.

You must develop your information resources to fit the following four criteria:

- *Timeliness:* Information must be provided with enough advanced notice so that it can be analyzed and reacted to. Late intelligence only frustrates.
- *Accuracy:* Few things are more embarrassing than a false start created by erroneous information. Develop information resources that have a proven track record of accuracy. The best information conduit is one for which you can independently verify its accuracy.
- *Relevancy:* For information to be useful it must have direct application to what you are doing. Unlike politicians such as Lyan Lobby who scoop up whatever tidbits they can with the hope that they find something of use, you must be discriminating. Expend your effort to develop beneficial information resources that help you do your job and keep you informed about the company and the industry. Such information sources include colleagues at competing firms, government agencies, university research centers, to name a few.
- *Discretion:* For information to be of use to you (as opposed to your rivals), it must not be generally known. You want your sources to provide information that can give you a leg up on the competition.

Computer Time and Equipment

Most companies use some sort of automated systems. Usually these have something to do with financial operations and possibly engineering and manufacturing. If you know how to use the information resources computers provide you will have an advantage over the likes of I. B. Meantuu. Meantuu never learned to use the computer because of the perceived threat they pose to his superiority. Locomotives can be heard to proclaim that they see no need to understand computers—that's what the bean counters are for.

The rest of us, however, need every resource advantage we can get. Computers present the following opportunities for you:

- *Information storage and retrieval:* Development of a good data base from which you can draw needed information quickly and easily will save you time. For example, if you are a salesman who writes many proposals, wouldn't it save you time if you were able to call up entire sections of previous winning proposals that are applicable to your current work?
- *Analytical capabilities:* Computers are very good at allowing you to quickly state a problem in mathematical terms and run various idea scenarios to predict probable outcomes. This can be done using any of the commercially available spread sheet programs (such as Lotus 1-2-3 from Lotus Development Corp.) that can crunch large amounts of information on small personal computers.
- *Organization:* Computers are great for helping get you organized. Simple-to-use specialty applications, such as mailing-list programs, can do everything from automating your Rolodex files to specifying materials needed for a particular job. Additionally, the new accounting software (specially programmed for non-accountants) can help keep your department on budget by tracking your expenditures against what you planned.

Computers also offer access to information through commercial data bases to which you can subscribe. Such information-retrieval services allow you to state the subject in which you are interested, then retrieve the most current periodical articles.

To the uninitiated, computers can be intimidating. This

will keep DIs like Imagonna Grabontoitz away because he doesn't have the time it takes to learn. Overcome your fear (if any) of computers and learn to use them. Take an introductory computer course at your local junior college or a short seminar at a computer store. Better yet, buy your own personal computer and learn to make it work for you.

Clout

Clout can be a source of power. Clout should also be treated as a resource used to get action when needed. When you fire your boss, you must obtain the clout your career requires to succeed. As your own boss, for example, you may not have the clout necessary to get a recalcitrant supplier to behave. You may, however, have a contact with the necessary clout. Knowing someone with clout who is willing to use it on your behalf is almost as good as having it yourself.

Silent clout rarely does you any good. You want people to be aware of your clout and your contacts. Watch how politically powerful people get things done. Clout works best on someone who responds to the *possibility* of its use rather than *actual* use. I have a client who has built up such powerful clout resources in his company that merely raising his eyebrows at peers and subordinates alike (they call it turning on the eyes) melts any reservations they may have had regarding his authority into warm Jell-O.

Eliza Collins, in *The Executive Dilemma* (John Wiley and Sons, New York, NY 1985), perceptively identifies the properties of clout as:

1. The ability to save a subordinate who is in trouble with the organization;
2. Influence and willingness to promote a talented subordinate;
3. Skill to get expenditures beyond those budgeted;

4. Tenacity to obtain above-average raises for deserving subordinates;
5. Ability to influence company policies and strategies;
6. Superiors seek the boss's advice and counsel;
7. Fast and direct access to superiors;
8. Well-connected. People with clout get early information about significant events and use it to further the organization's goals.

Does your present boss have any of these essentials of clout? Do you? For your boss to positively influence your career, he must carry some amount of clout.

Senior Management Attention

Do not overlook the attention senior management gives to you and your efforts, because it is another valuable resource. Such regard for your skills translates directly to a certain amount of power. Acclaim from management throughout the company gives you a wider audience and makes you less dependent on your boss for a fair evaluation of your worth and potential.

Lame Duk, the politician, carries his lust for management attention to an embarrassing degree. Most see right through Duk's apple-polishing. The difference between the way political grubs like Duk treat management attention and the way you do lies in the use of this resource. Lame seeks attention for his own self-aggrandizement. Duk has not learned that it is rare when you must indicate who is exactly responsible for the success or failure of a task. You should use the attention management pays to further aid you and your subordinates to do your jobs.

Relationships

Lyan Lobby perverts his relationships with others. There always seem to be ulterior motives for his friendships and alliances. Eventually all but the other politicians will evade Lobby, fearing that any relationship with him will be misinterpreted by those who really matter.

Your contacts and good relationships with others are a valuable resource. Treat them with respect, and give them the dignity they deserve. Do not abuse friendships both within and outside the company for personal gain. The best type of favor you can do for someone comes without having to be asked. Be helpful because it makes sense and it brings the company's ultimate goals that much closer. Help because you enjoy helping. Never do people favors just to set the hook for some future gain.

Solid relationships are built on a foundation of communication. Speak in a manner that communicates that you understand and share your listener's spirit and sentiments. Trust and confidence grow from the common ground you establish. People tend to better identify with you and elevate your status in their minds when they know and share where you are coming from.

Rewards

One of the most important resources for you to control are rewards. In our earlier example of Maggie the Scottie the reward was love and attention. For subordinates, the rewards tend to be of a more material class. If you are truly in charge you must have the reward resources at your command. These include performance reviews, ability to grant raises, promotions, vacations, and bonuses.

Before reward resources can work, the following criteria must be met:

• People must see the relation between their actions and the reward;
• People must want the reward and be motivated to get it;

- People must believe that you can obtain the reward for them.

There is an opposite and darker side to reward motivation: coercive stimulus (do this or else . . .). This works just the opposite of rewards and acts as a penalty. Though coercion can be a useful resource to draw upon in certain situations, it doesn't work as well as a positive reward.

Perceptions of Resources

Perceptions of your resources can be as important as the actual resources you command. This works especially well on people with whom you don't deal closely. Their exaggerated perception of the resources available to you can greatly enhance your power. This impression can be fostered with the trappings of office as used to the absurd by Tip Blabbermeister. I have been in Tip's office. It's ostentatious without being understated. He has a "wall of fame" on which he displays every diploma and certificate he ever earned (and some he probably did not). There are the pictures of Tip with every luminary, bigwig, and seminotable he has glad-handed. Leaping across another wall is the requisite stuffed marlin (likely purchased from a second-hand store). Behind his desk sits a credenza groaning under the weight of Tip's personal trophy collection (rumor has it that some belong to his son, Tip, Jr.). The place of honor is reserved for a bowling ball signed by all members of the 1973 tuna-canning league championship team (which Tip captained).

Your work area should say that you respect yourself and your surroundings, that you are neat and well-organized, and possibly a little something personal about you as well. Leave the garish displays to Blabbermeister. Your space should bespeak a subtle power along with the authority to command resources necessary to get your job done.

Given the choice to fight for and win resources such as a larger office, better equipment, and more people, take them. Do not hold back like Letsall Getalong, waiting for someone else to speak up. If they can be had, take the trappings and use them as a resource to expand your perceived image beyond what it would have been otherwise.

RESOURCES IDENTIFIED

Figure out what you need to complete a particular task. Then design a plan to obtain these resources. This plan should include:

- Timing for receipt of the necessary resources and how much your due date will slide if they are late;
- The quantity of each resource item and estimated costs to obtain them;
- The length of time you will need these resources. Be sure to include time for mid-course corrections and management review, PLUS an adequate contingency for unforeseen events such as equipment failure and repair.

Use the following procedure to specify in your plan what resources you require:

1. Plan what needs to be done and how it should be done.
2. Determine in a step-by-step fashion the major functions to be completed in order to achieve the objective.
3. Separate these major steps into specific tasks and assign people to each.
4. With the plan firmly in mind, list the resources needed for each step along with where to get them. Review

this list with the people who will execute it to be sure you have not missed something.

GET SCARCE RESOURCES

Resources come from a variety of locations, some from inside the company, others from places you would not expect. Large firms have formal allocation procedures. Such channels not only provide a formal way of procuring what you need to do your job, they usually furnish a tracking mechanism so the company knows who has what and for what purpose. Probably the most widely recognized formal resource channel is the budgeting process. This exercise allocates money to those who can demonstrate the most profitable use for it.

Proper Channels

Proper channels work for items requiring long lead times, such as major equipment purchases and personnel. Its strength is the approval process, which grinds through the organization. Its weakness, however, is its sluggishness. Know when to use proper channels and when to use other means to get badly needed resources.

Back Channels

The so-called back channels provide a less formal way of obtaining resources. Similar to a black market, back channels trade on deal making and calling in favors. Lyan Lobby and his political crowd are particularly adept at using back channels. For older companies the back channel has often become firmly entrenched as a means of obtaining resources.

Back channels require care to maintain and to use

effectively. Clout and influence oil the machinery that runs back channel operations. Senior management does not like the use of back channels because subordinates control it rather than those with approved authority. These secondary suppliers do not always allocate resources in a manner sanctioned by top management. The case of Oliver North and the Nicaraguan *contra* supply operation provides a case study of a back channel that was extremely effective but circumvented approved methods and laws.

Guerrilla Warfare

Sometimes referred to as the dirty-tricks squad, guerrilla warfare seeks to expropiate, commandeer, or otherwise snatch resources that should have gone to another application. Such methods can be rationalized by the fact that the company pays you to think, to be creative, and to get your job done rather than bow to bureaucratically induced failure. Of course, such tactics are done with the knowledge of as few people as possible.

I have known several "corporate guerrillas." One particularly enterprising lady, Kelly, needed two additional computer terminals in the branch office she managed. These terminals were not budgeted, but she purchased them and managed to stay in budget anyway. Kelly accomplished this feat by subleasing the extra 1,500 square feet of office space her branch didn't use. Her rental income produced a profit over the terminal costs, which was used to enhance her branch's profitability. Was this activity against corporate policy? Yes. Did the firm, as well as Kelly the "corporate guerrilla" benefit from her innovation? Also, yes. Was the corporate headquarters informed of this? Only after Kelly initiated a new policy of subleasing all excess space once she was promoted to regional manager.

Guerrilla tactics should be attempted only in the most

extreme circumstances. Being apprehended will mark you as one who has only his interests at heart (surprise, surprise) and as someone unwilling to play by the rules (they haven't yet guessed that you are rewriting the rules). The benefits can be bountiful, however, as seen by Colonel North's Nicaraguan supply operation, which not only used back channels but guerrilla warfare and anything else that got the job done. If you must use such methods, try not to overstep the limits of fair play too much and don't make it a habit. If the approved resource allocation procedures do not allow you to do your job, then change them within the system.

BENEFITS OF RESOURCES

Adequate resources provide power, clout, and independence from a boss who may be less savvy than you when it comes to supply-side economics. The pleaser, Letsall Getalong, provides a case in point. Competing successfully for scarce resources requires the firm belief that you are important and you can put these things to better use than others. Getalong willingly accepts such claims from juvenile competitors like Princess Rising Star. His subordinates are like poor waifs who must do without while the wicked stepsisters get the goodies.

The most useful benefit of providing your own resources can be seen in your lack of dependence on an inept boss to provide them for you. Excuses such as not having the proper tools are lame at best. The first question from an irate superior (and rightly so) will be, "Then why didn't you [expletive] get what you [expletive] needed?" This is a valid question, and it only makes things worse to point the finger at miserable Letsall Getalong, because it puts you in his class.

Another similar benefit of having your own resource

VIII

Four to Go:
Leading, Following,
and Steamrolling

"Jack, I know you don't want to take the heat if my idea fails. Still, I just know the chances of success are good. I believe in this approach so strongly that I'm going to risk it alone rather than possibly drag you down with me. If we don't get the contract I'll take full responsibility. I'm going to the old man myself, even though you disagree, and explain my idea. If I fall flat, then it's only me who has to answer."

Leadership continues to fascinate management psychologists. Many have tried to distill the common traits of leaders into simple formulas for success. Some suppose that leaders are born, not made. Others believe that leaders overflow with charisma. George Bernard Shaw once said that the only problem with Christianity is that no one practices its teachings. The same thing can be said of leadership. Many know the qualities of a good leader, yet few are able to habituate them.

Leading

When we speak of career leadership, we refer to guidance provided by that single person who has a realistic vision of your goals along with the plan, tenacity, and resourcefulness to get you there. Of course only one person has such intimate knowledge: you.

Following

Self-centered bosses, such as the locomotive and DI, seem to forget one of the most important traits of a good leader: knowing how to be a good follower. Have you seen the boss who asks for an opinion, then interrupts the answer, saying, "You know what I think?" Only the best leaders are secure in their own leadership role and smart enough to know when to follow a colleague or subordinate who has an idea worth pursuing. Part of leading people means that you do not smother the abilities and talents of those being led.

Steamrolling

Steamrolling means that you have no choice but to surge right over your boss to seize control over your career. Such action does not endear you to the boss but may become necessary when dealing with the disorganized incompetent or Lyan Lobby, the politician. For you to lead yourself as well as your boss and subordinates, you must understand what makes a good leader and what kind of leadership abilities you must develop.

LEADERSHIP V. CHARISMA

Don't confuse leadership ability with charisma. There are many charismatic people who could not lead their way out of a paper bag. You may be working for one. Many people are born with charisma. Charismatic leaders, however, are usually all fluff. They would rather look good than be good and usually don't last. Political bosses rely on charisma to get them through. True leaders, however, earn the respect of their superiors, peers, and subordinates. They are always searching for ways to further develop their leadership abilities. Conferring the title of boss on someone doesn't automatically make him or her a leader. Effective leaders are chiseled from the hard rock of experience and possess an unflinching belief in themselves and their abilities.

How many bosses have you seen who relish their ability to make subordinates quake in their boots without saying a word? Managers who lead by such intimidation will have a short-lived tenure at best. Their subordinates will put up with such incompetence for as long as it takes them to find a better job. Don't confuse the ability to lead with the ability to induce fear.

There is a difference between being mean and being tough. Don't write off tough bosses. Andrew S. Grove correctly observed in his book *One-on-One with Andy Grove:*

"It is a lot harder to be tough than it is to be mean. A tough-minded manager can reason his way to the correct course of action rather than take the easy way out. A tough manager, like a good coach, drives the team to outstanding performance, demands a lot from his players, spurs them on, praises and criticizes them to reach a common goal."

Tough managers are respected and often admired. General George Patton had a reputation as an extremely tough officer. Yet he was also one of our country's most effective leaders.

Once you have fired your boss and taken responsibility for the leadership of your job and career yourself, develop a combination of enough charisma to keep people interested but a tough outlook on your mission and how you intend to achieve your goals.

LEADERSHIP

There are many definitions of leadership. *The Random House Collegiate Dictionary* has more than twenty. Leaders guide, conduct, influence, and induce things to happen. Most leaders are also achievers. Their past and anticipated future achievements produce faith in their abilities.

Professional partnerships such as law firms, public accounting firms, and consulting firms are notorious for having poor leadership. Partners are often promoted without substantive management skills or a clue as to how to lead people. Consequently, they try to derive authority from their rank. This can be particularly aggravating when dealing with juvenile bosses such as Princess Rising Star. Effective leaders encourage people to accept their ideas because they're sound. Likewise, they are willing to accept subordinate's ideas because they make sense. Real leaders do not browbeat their subordinates with the club of their office.

Leaders are successful because they are achievers. Likewise, achievers attain their goals partly because of their leadership abilities. The qualities of both leadership and a solid achievement orientation produce a powerful formula for success.

Properties of Leadership

Achievement-oriented leaders possess such qualities as:

- *People focus:* This means that the leader centers more on others than on himself (almost impossible for Lyan Lobby and Princess Rising Star). Excellent communication skills and positive thinking are two most obvious traits. Additionally, people orientation makes a leader the most enthusiastic cheerleader for the subordinate.

- *Courage:* Leaders stand up not only for their beliefs and ideas but for their subordinates when faced with unwarranted criticism from other bosses. Additionally, leaders are secure in their faith in themselves—so much so that they are not afraid to take risks. Should they fail, their past and future success will more than compensate for a short-term loss.

- *Judgment:* The serious leader exhibits consistently good judgment. She does not back away from decisions. Instead she weighs the pros and cons, makes the best decision she can, and does not second-guess herself.

- *Tenacity and resoucefulness:* Good leaders know what they want, and they know how to get it. A leader/achiever takes responsibility to deliver the goods and does just that. Such people think beyond the obvious. They don't fear difficult tasks and immediately consider damage control measures as does Tip Blabbermeister. Rather, they anticipate the challenge and optimize the potential benefits. John and Robert Kennedy were such resourceful leaders. One of Robert Kennedy's most powerful speeches included a paraphrase from George Bernard Shaw: "When others ask, Why, I ask, Why not?" Such is the conviction of a true leader.

- *Vision:* Leaders have a good idea of how they wish to shape future events and are able to persuade others that not only are they right but that their goals are worth pursuing. The untrained boss fails to connect current events with future impacts on themselves, their jobs, and companies, as well as their subordinates. Visionaries look for and exploit synergistic situations where the sum of the parts, when combined, exceeds the value of the parts taken separately.

- *Capability diligently applied:* It was Sydney Harris who said, "Mere diligence can never do in a dozen years what talent does in a day; yet at the same time, talent without diligence keeps squandering its inheritance and soon goes bankrupt." Leaders know that they either magnify or blunder away the trust of their subordinates whenever they open their mouths. Leaders know that anything worth getting involved in is worth doing to the best of their capabilities. Subordinates and bosses alike learn to trust and rely on that one hundred percent commitment.

- *Enthusiasm:* Leaders and achievers approach their jobs and their commitments to their subordinates with an almost ferocious enthusiasm. They are always striving and trying to find ways to help their subordinates excel beyond what they ordinarily would achieve. The emotional peaks and valleys found in the DI and pleaser are not evident in the leader/achiever. Rather, they are on more of an even keel, usually up.

- *Power and risk:* Leaders truly believe in themselves and their vision. They seek the power to get what needs to be done to achieve their goals. Additionally, they have such confidence in themselves and their judgment that they don't fear taking risks. Even if they should fail, they know they have the resourcefulness and diligence to extricate themselves and their subordinates.

- *Empathy:* Effective leaders experience the feelings others may have when placed in a similar situation. They frequently ask (and correctly answer) the question, "What would I do if I were in her shoes?" From such empathy, a leader can determine the most effective way to help a subordinate perform to the standards they both expect.

These are some of the traits you should exhibit to take charge of your own career. Chances are, if you recognize the need to fire your boss, you have discovered for yourself a serious lacking in some or all of these areas on the part of your boss.

Characteristics of a Competent Follower

Think of a leader as the navigator. He conjures up what distant lands the voyage will seek. The follower becomes the tactician whose job turns to building the boat and loading provisions for the journey. There is nothing wrong with being a follower. Many successful followers have recognized that maybe they aren't cut out to be great leaders, but they make superb number twos. The problem comes, however, when a born follower thinks for some reason that he should be a leader and tries to impose that role on himself, his boss, and his subordinates. I. B. Meantuu, the locomotive, probably started off as a potential leader. When it became obvious to his bosses that I. B. had restrictions that limited further ascension, he was derailed from the fast track and left to stagnate in his present job. But no one told I. B. he would go no farther, and he has not reconciled himself to the obvious. Consequently he has become a locomotive using all the brute force, temper tantrums, and holier-than-thou attitudes available in his arsenal. Because of his management style, his subordinates have become frustrated with the locomotive taking them on a trip to nowhere.

Recognize follower traits in yourself and your boss. Use these features to your advantage and augment them with some of the leadership characteristics shown earlier. Here are some traits with which you can identify the follower:

- *Capable, but less so than leaders:* Followers are not necessarily incompetent. As long as they are not thrust into a situation where they are forced to lead, followers can do their jobs very capably. In fact, some of the best number twos resist being promoted to roles of leadership because they know their limitations.

- *Commitment and risk:* Followers, especially pleasers like Letsall Getalong, remain uncommitted until the leader appears or the risk of commitment can be shared with the group. Politicians like Lame Duk will remain uncommitted unless they see a situation that can be exploited for personal gain. Politicians look for parades to jump in front of and lead.

- *Respected by all and revered by many:* The follower tends to make friends rather than enemies. Aside from a frustrating inability to make decisions, followers are less controversial and more liked than their leaders. Followers want to be "one of the guys." They find safety and security in the camaraderie of a group.

- *Fatalistic:* Followers have a realistic grasp on what they can influence and what they cannot. Things that appear to the follower beyond their ability to control are left to either the leader or to fate. The leader, on the other hand, will find a way to change an event if it affects his goals. Lack of such resolve certainly makes for a less stressful life.

LEADERSHIP ACTIVITIES

There are specific things the effective leader does to enhance her position. These activities both establish her dominant role and assist her subordinates in doing the things necessary to achieve the leader's vision. Observe your boss and see if he or she does any of the following things, which make for an effective leader.

- *Time and attention:* Bosses and leaders are employed to provide sufficient time and attention to their subordinates. Hurriup N. Wate, the DI, never seems to have enough time. She's always running from crisis to crisis, never allowing either herself or her subordinates to catch their breath. Further, Wate's disorganization means that otherwise efficient subordinates are made less so by the boss.

  True leaders will take the necessary time to communicate the task, make needed mid-course corrections, and review the final product so that all can share the group's success.

- *Training:* Leaders spend time training subordinates in the fundamentals of their jobs. Further training beyond that will come when needed and only *if* needed. Locomotive bosses like I. B. Meantuu never seem satisfied with how their subordinates have learned the job and are constantly reteaching.

  Effective leaders demonstrate faith in their teaching abilities as well as in the intelligence of their subordinates by resigning from the role as teacher and taking up the job of coach and cheerleader as soon as possible.

- *Evaluation of performance:* Effective leaders objectively judge their subordinates' performance and suggest ways to improve. Criticism remains on a professional, rather than personal, level and is always intended for constructive purposes rather than to enhance the authority of the boss.

Letsall Getalong, the pleaser, can be particularly dangerous when evaluating his subordinates' performance. Pleasers place their own convenience and personal preferences over their job responsibilities and obligation to their subordinates. Getalong seduces his subordinates into a false sense of security. When it comes time for a promotion or a raise, it often comes as a shock to a worker when Letsall tells him that there was something drastically wrong. Unfortunately, by this time, it is too late.

- *Sincere encouragement:* I. B. Meantuu, the locomotive, can make a compliment sound like a slap in the face. An effective leader, however, remains secure in his own role and genuinely needs his subordinates to succeed at their tasks for him to succeed at his. Encouragement and coaching comes from a heartfelt sincerity, which gets communicated to his people. Unlike I. B., who will jump in and do a subordinate's job himself at the slightest provocation, the true leader draws a line between his job and that of his subordinates. Just as a coach cannot play the game himself, neither should a leader do a subordinate's job.

- *Communication:* Leaders make time to talk with their people, whether about a customer problem or about their careers. Leaders judge the effectiveness of their communication not by what they got out of it, but by what the subordinate received. They elicit feedback as to how the subordinate feels about what was discussed. Misunderstandings are cleared up immediately. The politician Tip Blabbermeister fails to develop confidence among his staff. They fear that something they tell him can and will be used against them at Tip's first self-serving opportunity.

Effective communication means having the confidence in your boss that you can bring him bad news as well as good news without having your head chewed off.

If your boss falls short in most of these leadership activities, it's time to get a new boss. When you take over that responsibility, make sure that you practice the activities of leaders—first on yourself as your own supervisor, then, as you rise up the ladder of success, on your own subordinates.

The Leader's Job

Again, Eliza Collins, in her book *The Executive Dilemma,* insightfully presents three characteristics found in most jobs held by acknowledged leaders. Compare these three aspects of a leader's job with your boss's position and with yours.

- *Relevancy:* Most leaders' jobs are important to the goals of the firm and will have a major influence on the firm's success.
- *Discretion:* The leader's job cannot be done by rote procedures. Leaders are paid for their judgment, flexibility, and adaptation of innovative approaches to problem solving. Upper management gives leaders the latitude to exercise their best judgment. In fact, respect for a person's judgment goes a long way toward making him or her a leader.
- *Recognition:* Leaders generally hold highly visible positions and command the attention of other key individuals in the organization—not surprising, since leaders are generally responsible for functions that

greatly influence the success of the company. Further, they are allowed to use their own judgment rather than the collective wisdom of the overall management team.

If your boss fails to use (or is not allowed to use) her own discretion, if she has not become visible to those who count within the company, and if you see her function as inconsequential to the firm's overall success, the likelihood that she will competently help your career along a successful path should be obvious. When you fire your boss and become responsible for your own career, you must position yourself to take a leadership role, which includes making your position relevant, using discretion, and attaining recognition.

USES AND ABUSES OF POWER

Theodore Roosevelt said, "Power undirected by high purpose spells calamity, and high purpose by itself is utterly useless if the power to put it into effect is lacking."

People who have power disclaim its existence. People who crave power try to hide their hunger. People who engage in power schemes (Lyan Lobby, the political boss, still the grand master) do so secretly. Power in the workplace can be effectively used to accomplish the mission; if used incompetently or not at all, it will undermine the process. Many people who feel their boss needs to be fired from their careers cite power abuse as one of the reasons for his or her failure as a boss.

Bosses who are charged with accountability and responsibility for a task without the power or resources to complete the job cause frustration and, ultimately, failure. Such lack of power breeds bossiness rather than true leadership. Letsall Getalong, the pleaser, falls into this category. Rather than confront his own boss and demand the resources to do his job or refuse to be held accountable, he weakly accepts what soon becomes an impossible situation. Additionally, Letsall fears alienating people by using his power. To prevent this, he pushes responsibility and authority down to those who should not have it. When the resulting decisions are appealed back up the ladder to him, he usually just echoes the original decision made and tells the antagonists to work it out among themselves.

Juvenile bosses like our Princess Rising Star often are too inexperienced or uncertain of their positions to use their power effectively. These two types of bosses lose the respect of their subordinates when it becomes evident that they have the responsibility without the clout to get the job done. In either case, a powerless boss can do your career a great deal of harm when it comes time for raises and promotions.

Power can be broadly defined to include such things as authority, contacts, clout, responsibility, and resources. A manager's power undergoes a constant ebb and flow like a tidal cycle. The more important a particular job to the success of their firm, the more power the person responsible wields. As a particular task winds up, management's attention often turns to other areas of the company, thus reducing the influence and power of the boss. The contacts a boss has affect the power he enjoys. A boss having an excellent working relationship with a powerful executive who was just arrested for embezzlement will suffer a significant loss of influence (perhaps his job as well).

Bosses who control resources tend to be among the most powerful people in an organization. But the importance of resources tends to shift over time. Scarce commodities that suddenly become easier to find or become of less importance will erode the power of the person who distributes them.

An often seen adjunct to real power is called referent

power. This describes the essence of power as defined by Tip Blabbermeister. Referent power revolves around one's association with those who possess real power in the hope that some of it will rub off on them.

Be aware of the power structure in your organization. Determine where both you and your boss reside on the power curve. Anticipate where your boss's power will be when you need her. Consider where her power base comes from using such things as responsibility, resources, contacts, and influence as indexes.

Power Channels

How does leadership translate to power? There are three channels through which leaders funnel power and clout to accomplish their goals:

- *Supply channels:* Material, money, people, resources, and rewards comprise the main supplies leaders need to accomplish their tasks. Effective managers focus their power on obtaining the right combination of supplies at the right time so that their organization can do its job without interruption and within the time required.

- *Information channels:* Information and its timing provide the leader with power to run the organization. The confidence people have in their boss comes partly as a result of trust that the boss has all intelligence necessary to guide the group toward succeeding at its task. Judicious use of information derived from formal channels as well as (and probably more importantly) informal back channels gives the leader a definite leg up. In this area Lame Duk, our politician from Peking, excels. The problem, however, evolves from Lame's failure to use his information for the good of the group. Instead, he hoards it to be used later for personal gain.

- *Support channels:* The leader's power base derives

from the support he gets from the company's movers and shakers. Leaders are known for innovation, taking initiative, and for not being risk averse. For a leader to do these things, he must have upper-level support. Further, because many of his projects are time sensitive, he cannot be restrained by having to go through a formal approval process. The most successful and powerful leaders enjoy such trust from management that they have carte blanche to act on their own initiative with little or no intervention from above.

TECHNIQUES OF LEADERSHIP, FOLLOWERSHIP, AND STEAMROLLING

Knowing when to lead, follow, or steamroll your boss provides a skill that will come in handy when you fire your boss from your career.

When to Lead

The time to lead comes when the boss fails to take the initiative or when the leadership he does provide takes you in a direction that will not enhance your objectives. Some bosses are more likely to fail as leaders than others. Pleasers such as Letsall Getalong allow themselves to be swept away by the strongest current. Such leadership by committee results in disjointed objectives and little coordinated effort. Alternately, politicians such as Tip Blabbermeister do provide a type of leadership. Unfortunately it goes in the wrong direction. Instead of leading the group toward its goals where all can share in the achievement, Tip's main concern is leading Tip to greener pastures.

When to Follow

Following locomotives such as I. B. Meantuu or juveniles such as Princess Rising Star can be painful. Yet they can also help you achieve your goals. Following such bosses necessitates sharing control over specific parts of your job. By doing this, you lessen the emotional trauma to which an abusive locomotive often subjects his underlings and still allow yourself the benefit of his experience and background. This can be equally important with someone such as Rising Star. You need to learn just what she has that makes her so outstanding. Position yourself so that you can be swept into her updraft. At the same time, you must insulate yourself from her preoccupation with her own advancement.

When to Steamroll

Steamrolling means that you have placed the boss in a position where no alternative exists other than to swallow your demands for greater authority, less supervision, more responsibilities, and higher recognition. Steamrolling implies a power struggle between your boss and yourself.

When DIs such as Imagonna Grabontoitz adversely affect your career with their incompetence and when they insist on retaining every ounce of control, you have no choice but to challenge them for leadership of your job. Sometimes this turns into a win-or-lose contest with the subordinate usually coming up short. Even so, if you see no future where you are and your best efforts to fire your boss from your career don't help, you are probably better off working for someone else whose management abilities won't stifle your progress.

Decision by group consensus works well to steamroll over an obdurate boss. Letsall Getalong, the pleaser, will have a hard time disagreeing with a course of action to which each one of his staff has agreed. Further, when the boss's boss lends her support to greater responsibility among the subordinates, it's hard to say she doesn't know what she's talking about.

LEADERSHIP TECHNIQUES FOR
DIFFERENT TYPES OF BOSSES

Regardless of the type of boss you have, try putting yourself in his or her place. Identify:

1. What the *BOSS* perceives as your motivations;
2. His hidden agenda;
3. What *HE* thinks you want him to do;
4. The fears or restrictions the boss has that might limit or prevent him from doing what you want;
5. Whether he sees this as a power struggle.

If you get stuck and can't seem to get through to the boss, voice your concerns and solicit his feelings. If the boss has a hard time admitting that he oversupervises and in fact at times does the work himself, read this back as, "In other words, you're saying that you are concerned that quality will drop if anybody other than you does the job?"

Control the discussion and listen firmly. Let the boss know that you are interested and she should be, too. Don't let the boss prattle on about inconsequential topics not germane to your point. If the boss gets on a roll so that you can't get a word in edgeways, regain control with a simple nod of the head and a snappy, "I can appreciate that," followed up in the same breath with the beginning of your point.

Here are some suggestions for use when dealing with the various types of bosses:

Locomotive

I. B. Meantuu, like most locomotives, believes he has all the answers and he won't suffer fools gracefully. When you lay down the law in terms of the extent of supervision you need, the detail of the instructions you require, and the authority you must have to do your job independently, he may perceive that you want to usurp his power. Assure him that you both can come out winners by delegating some of his responsibilities to you. He will have more time, you will get the opportunity to learn a new aspect of the business and grow professionally, etc.

Avoid position bargaining. This means that one of you must accept the other's position. Position bargaining implies a win/lose outcome. A locomotive won't jump the tracks unless he can come out ahead by doing so. Show him how.

Politicians

Politicians condemn motivations and intentions. Because political hacks like Lyan Lobby have devious methods and hidden agendas themselves, they automatically suspect others of the same behavior. Gain Lyan's confidence by honestly laying your cards on the table. Tell him why you feel the need to begin making your own job decisions. Remember, you are dealing with a true professional, one who can spot a novice from afar.

When talking with Lobby, speak his language. Even though it may be the blunt truth, resist saying such things as, "You broke your word." Instead, describe the issue in terms of how it makes you feel, such as, "I feel let down. . . ." Guide masters of the game such as Tip Blabbermeister toward suggesting ways in which you can both achieve what you each want from your jobs. After all, subordinates who are self-sufficient on the job and competent to run things without intervention from the boss are walking testimonials to the boss's excellence as a manager. Lead Tip into reaching this conclusion for himself.

Politicians are concerned with saving face (preferably

their own). You should propose a solution that gets you where you want to be and at the same time makes the boss look good. To do otherwise invites a hasty rejection.

Disorganized Incompetent

A disorganized incompetent such as Hurriup N. Wate may be so busy creating turmoil that she cannot hear you say there's a better way. Nevertheless, get her attention you must.

DIs are sensitive. Don't antagonize them by attacking the person (tempting though it may be). Instead, stick with the issues. Imagonna Grabontoitz will try to weasel out of a commitment by consenting to study the problem and "get back to you." Stop her. Present a series of well thought-out solutions (that work and will get you what you want), which you can sell on the spot, gain concurrence, and move on.

Pleasers

Letsall Getalong will do much of your work for you, given half a chance. Let him do what he does best—compromise. This time, however, you won't cave in. Insist on the resources you need to gain complete control over your job so you are no longer dependent on someone content with substandard results. If Getalong wants you to share responsibility with someone else and you know that way to be less than optimal, stonewall the boss.

Getting upset with many boss types rarely works. With locomotives like I. B. Meantuu, it only becomes a contest of who can yell the loudest. The pleaser, however, can't stand to have angry subordinates. Especially subordinates who are angry at him. With Getalong, a little well-placed hostility can go a long way. Further, after the dust has settled and you are operating more effectively without the boss's help, whatever hard feelings that developed are usually forgotten.

Juveniles

Most parents have survived the curfew issue with their teenagers. The question of how late children can stay out accounts for only the tip of the iceberg. Buried somewhere under the adolescent posturing and tears lie such torments as peer pressure, acknowledging that they are responsible people rather than children, and the urge to exert control over their environment as well as authority figures. The same thing holds true for juvenile bosses.

Leading Princess Rising Star as you would the pleaser will not work. She is smarter and has a firmer grasp of her goals than Getalong. Do not contest the Princess for control over lesser aspects of your job. A certain amount of oversupervising, though it may be irritating, can be temporarily tuned out if need be. Guide Princess into a management style that suits both of you, then follow her.

Guidance can come from suggestions that she manage in a specific way, that she delegate responsibilities for particularly good reasons, which you supply. Remember Star's primary motivation: eventual ascension to supreme ruler. She cannot accomplish that without first designating an heir apparent to her own throne and without demonstrating the ability to lead people. Her ambitions require her to develop subordinates as fast as she herself unfolded. Make sure that you are there to provide living proof of Star's ability to grow self-sufficient, creative, responsible managers who are ready for additional responsibilities and promotion. This way, you both come out winners.

IX

Conspire Against Your Boss: Putting Theory into Practice

Conspiracy almost sounds like a dirty word. It invites images of dubious figures skulking about dark shadows with apocalyptic intentions. Yet when you take steps to fire an incompetent boss from your career, you do indeed form a conspiracy of sorts. The final outcome, however, will likely be that both you and your boss reach a better position than you would have otherwise. Further, this conspiracy will be carried out in the open with the full knowledge and approval (if you've done your homework) of your boss.

The conspiracy required to effectively fire your boss from your career involves a definite plan of action and the recruitment of several key individuals (your boss included) to act as accessories. Your accomplices will provide some of the expertise, the clout, and the access to resources necessary to triumph over your boss, which you may lack in the beginning. With a little planning and some common sense, the conspiracy you head to fire your boss does not have to be something dark and evil. Instead, you will develop a respected image of concern about your career and a willingness to take on the responsibilities of a better position.

The story of Lisa Goldsworthy, illustrated below, shows how one subordinate determined that her boss needed to be fired from her career. We examine the steps she takes to formulate a plan that effectively quashes the problems presented by her unfit boss. The case surveys her moves aimed at limiting damage and eventually overcoming the obstacles of working for an inept boss. You will see how many of the techniques described in earlier chapters are put into practice by our imaginary subordinate.

TESTING GOLDSWORTHY'S METTLE

Acme Products Corporation touts itself as a tiny island of excellence in an ocean of mediocre office furniture. The four partners who comprise Acme's management team divide responsibilities along the lines of their own areas of expertise: sales, finance, manufacturing, and engineering. Lisa Goldsworthy has worked for a year and a half as one of five salespeople under I. A. Tollah, the partner responsible for sales and marketing. The action picks up as Goldsworthy comes into the office from yet another successful sales presentation.

"Goldsworthy! Goldsworthy, get in here," comes the irresistible mandate from partner I. A. Tollah's office.

"You bellowed?" quakes Lisa, trying to appear unruffled as she saunters into her boss's office.

"How'd it go with your interior designers? I never was sold on going to those hustlers who try to scalp us on price, then mark up the goods to their clients by fifty percent. Ya know, if you'd have listened to me, you wouldn't be wasting your time. . . ."

"I got the sale," Goldsworthy interrupts before her boss's diatribe gathers steam. "They bought five workstations and three executive setups," she falters, hoping this will set him in his place.

"Well, five workstations don't carry enough profit to buy my cigars this month. You got to learn to sell the high margin stuff. What we have here is a failure to communicate. When I was president of Gibson & Rude back in '63 I got my salesmen movin' by . . ." Lisa turns on her spike heels and storms out the door without giving her boss the satisfaction of finishing his haggard war story.

Analysis

Tollah hit the nail on the head. They both have a failure to communicate. Clearly Lisa Goldsworthy has a problem boss. Lisa must decide how best to limit the damage I. A. can inflict on her career and personal life. The first step centers around identification of the type of boss.

From the scenario so far, we know several things about I. A. Tollah:

1. Lisa had just done what she's paid for—make a sale. Yet before he even heard how her presentation went, Tollah began his critique. This guy lacks the sensitivity we normally associate with a toad.

2. Without missing a beat, upon hearing of her success the boss told her it was not good enough.

3. Rather than help, her boss has taken the position that he knows her approach will not work and he's just waiting for confirmation.

4. Reference to his presidency "back in '63" indicates nostalgia for the days of power. It also begs the question of what happened and why he now is only one of four partners in an "also ran" firm. From this, Tollah's career has probably settled into a downward spiral. Certainly he has little upward mobility.

5. From what we've heard of this despot, it can be

assumed that he manages with brute force rather than any leadership ability.

You are right if you pegged Tollah as a locomotive boss. Certainly, he's not a pleaser! Let's pick up Lisa's dinner conversation that evening.

"Drew, you know it upsets me to talk about work," Lisa snappishly replies to a cheery "how was your day" from her husband. "I just don't know what to do about old I. A. Tollahassahola. He criticizes me for selling what few of our products are competitive because they're not profitable. Yet our stuff is so overengineered, you could drive a tank over it without a scratch. No wonder the company can't make any money. He's prejudiced against working with interior-design firms rather than the end user. That man doesn't yet realize that sixty-five percent of all offices with more than ten thousand square feet of space use professional designers."

"Uh-huh, well, gee . . ."

"Don't you patronize me, Drew. I can't take it from you, too. . . ."

Analysis

Husband Drew is the unfortunate victim of spill-over from Lisa's job. She takes her frustration home with her and transfers her anger from Tollah, who won't listen, to Drew, who has no choice. If Tollah dispenses such criticism to her face, imagine what I. A. tells his partners about Lisa behind her back.

Lisa has allowed an incompetent boss to place her in a failing position. Her salary will never increase beyond meager raises because she's doing nothing to cause a quantum leap in her value to the firm. Because of her antagonism, Lisa won't allow Tollah to teach her anything. With his almost certain criticism of her to the other partners, there can be little hope for Lisa's advancement within the company. Her career will flounder without significant change.

Conclusion

Lisa must remove the stifling instructions, excessive supervision, and personal criticism from her career. By firing her boss, Lisa can be free to develop her own following within the firm. She can do this while retaining the help provided by Tollah's experience, contacts, resources, and technical expertise.

Once she decided to fire her boss, Lisa methodically developed a scheme to get it done. Her plan included four main goals: (1) Remove immediately the most distressing aspects of working for I. A. Tollah, (2) Become an expert in an area where Tollah has little experience and use that niche to create a separate identity for herself, (3) Dominate Tollah and make him dependent on her newly found expertise, (4) Consolidate her power base and move completely away from her old boss.

Lisa carried out each step with the determination of someone possessed. She was smart enough to realize that her corporate survival as well as that of her personal life depended on her ability to remove the demon from her career. Here's how she implemented her scheme.

AX I. A. TOLLAH

Tollah seemed to see his role as the chaperon of his department. This antagonized Lisa, who felt that she was beyond such intense supervision, especially from someone she believed was not up to the challenge. Tollah's management style left little room for creativity. Lisa came to grips with this one afternoon when she arranged a private meeting with Tollah. She insisted that they meet in her office after quitting time.

"Thanks for coming, Mr. Tollah. I've wanted to have this talk with you for some time now. We are just not working as a team. I'm not doing as well as I know I can, and I'm sure not getting the benefit of your years of experience. Frankly, if something does not change very soon, I'm going to begin looking for another job."

Tollah stared at her from behind puffy eyes, over his several chins, and blinked for a minute. He expected a repeat of their run-in last week, ending with her fleeing like a scared rabbit. Instead, he found himself peering at a Lisa Goldsworthy whose spine was no longer made of Jell-O. Because she didn't show any signs of backing down and because her calm, authoritative tone was not lost even on him, he responded, "Why, Lisa, you know my door is always open to all my salesMEN [emphasis, Tollah's]. I'm here to help. Tell me, what can I do for you?" He was making his usual attempt to remain in control. It usually worked. He couldn't understand what had changed.

"You are a better salesperson than you are a supervisor, Mr. Tollah. You find it difficult to believe that we will do our jobs without your domineering oversight of every detail of our work." Without mincing words Lisa continued to calmly describe her boss's shortcomings and how they diminished her performance. When she was through, she had shown Tollah exactly how she intended to begin supervising herself, how her customer call records would be kept open for review whenever I. A. wanted to see them, and how she intended to exceed her sales quota. She identified the markets and customers she intended to attack and quantified her sales targets for each. She described how she planned to work efficiently (doing things right the first time) and work effectively (doing the right things).

She ended with, "Mr. Tollah, what I propose is this: Give

me one month on my own using the techniques I've just described. I guarantee my sales will be up ten percent over what they are now. I'll keep you informed of how I'm doing, and I'll seek your advice when I need it. Just one month, Mr. Tollah. I need freedom to grow. Someone gave you the chance once, that's how you developed your style and why you've achieved the success you have. Now I'm in the same position you were twenty-five years ago. Please return the break someone once gave you."

Faced with Goldsworthy's overwhelming commitment and her reasonable plan of attack, he walked straight through the door Lisa left open. "OK, one month, and I'll be very interested to see how you do." He felt certain that Lisa would fail and thus verify the effectiveness of his management abilities. Besides, then he could be rid of this thorn in his side once and for all.

The Goldsworthy Touch

Due to I. A. Tollah's prejudice against courting interior designers, none of Acme's five salespeople had any contacts in this area, except Lisa. Her research showed that larger, wealthier companies used a designer for their offices more often than not and that this figure had been rising at an increasing rate for the past several years. Lisa had already decided that concentration on the design trade would become her niche. She had met some of the principals of the more successful firms in the city. Additionally, she had written a short article on space-saving workstations for users of computer terminals. The trade magazine containing Lisa's article hit the newsstands during her test month. She reprinted the article and sent it out to every potential client she could think of.

Lisa pounded the phones. She called every design firm in the city, introduced herself, and asked for an appointment.

She got ten appointments and was put on the bidder's list for five projects. While doing her proposals, she came up with some ideas that enhanced the overall design and reduced cost for three of the projects. She personally presented her ideas to her potential customers.

After the first week, she invited Tollah into her office for a progress report.

"Can't say as I've seen any more sales from you, Lisa," he began while shaping his fingers into a steeple as he did when he knew he had the upper hand. "Haven't seen you in the office much, either, come to think of it. Where you been, girl?"

"Mr. Tollah, you gave me a month, barely a week has gone by. I've been out of the office meeting my clients. Here's the list of calls I've made along with the results of each. When I'm not out meeting clients, I'm next door in the finance department where they have the computers I need to do the proposals I've been invited to submit. Remember, you refused to get us computers. You said they were no substitute for the personal touch," she told him, all the while smiling. "Finally, you haven't seen me because when I do get back to the office, it's so late, everyone else has gone home."

"Well, I suppose if you throw enough against the wall, some of it's bound to stick. Still, I thought I'd see something by now."

"Good things come to those with patience, Mr. Tollah."

Lisa and Tollah had similar conversations over the next two weeks. Finally, during the fourth week, Lisa was notified that two of her proposals had been accepted and the purchase contracts were signed.

"Time's up, Lisa. You promised you would have your sales up by now. What can you show me?" Tollah asked, tapping his foot against the chair leg, waiting for what he fully expected to be an admission of failure.

"So it is," an exasperated Goldsworthy admitted. "Two of the bids I made were accepted. That, along with my other business, increased my sales over last month only eight percent. You win, Mr. Tollah. I guess I'm not as good as I thought."

"What happened to the other three bids you made? Why didn't you get 'em?"

"On one I was beaten by lower pricing and the other, by faster delivery. The third was to Space Systems Corp., which hasn't made a decision yet."

"Space Systems, eh," he muttered, reaching for the phone and dialing a number from memory. "Bubba, I. A. here. Now, Bubba, you jes' listen up. . . ." When the conversation ended, Tollah nodded to Lisa and said, "There, you got your ten percent sales increase. Bubba Morton's the chairman of SSC and a good old boy I know from back home. He just needed a little pushing is all, and I'm just the SOB to do it," he said chuckling in obvious triumph. Tollah leaned toward Lisa in his most confidential manner and said that he never saw one of his salesMEN (emphasis still Tollah's) work as hard as she had over the last month. He said that his management style had worked for twenty-five years, but on his best day, he could not have motivated someone to work like Lisa had nor produce the results she did.

From then on, Lisa remained self-supervising. She still had to report to Tollah, and he still took most of the credit for her improved performance. But at least he stopped oversupervising and seemed to regard Goldsworthy with a little more respect. She stopped dreading contact with the boss and learned how to use him as a resource rather than trying to ignore him. They both began doing their real jobs, rather than each other's.

Goldsworthy's Specialty

Lisa realized that if she was to become independent of Tollah, she must further develop this area of expertise unfamiliar to her boss. She would use this niche to create a separate identity for herself. During the ensuing three months Lisa took two courses in basic interior design at the local university extension. She wanted to be able to converse with her target market in their own language.

She further defined her area of specialty to be those designers who concentrate in high-technology office environments, which employ mostly professionals. She felt her company's existing product lines to be best suited to this niche. Finally, she became familiar with some of the computer software dedicated to interior design. One in particular allowed her to lay out entire office environments, then move around furniture, plants, even entire walls with the touch of a button.

To pursue her specialty niche she identified those areas of the country that had an increasing population of high-tech companies. Until now, her firm had just been a regional company. She realized, however, that the narrower her specialization, the larger had to be the potential market. A search through a computerized on-line data base revealed six target markets: Los Angeles; the area around San Francisco known as Silicon Valley; Huntsville, Alabama; southern Florida; Scottsdale, Arizona; and Houston.

From the same data base, she obtained the names, addresses, and phone numbers of each of the design firms located in these six areas.

Goldsworthy Sets the Pace

Lisa was smart enough to realize that her separate identity from I. A. Tollah required her to set new trends, not follow the same old saw espoused by her (now former) boss. Here's what she did:

- The company had no catalog or brochure that defined Lisa's specialty and targeted her new market. She created one herself using desktop publishing software and the computers in the finance department. She mailed the catalog along with her article to each of her prospects.

- Again she pounded the phones. One week after her new brochures hit her prospects' offices, she called each one of them, introduced herself, and asked about their current projects. Five did indeed have engagements that could use Lisa's expertise and products. She was asked to submit a bid for each of these jobs.

- Goldsworthy convinced her boss to set a small section of the company showroom aside for her high-tech displays.

- Lisa determined that she was a contender for three of the contracts on which she bid. She made arrangements to fly these three prospective customers and their designers in to see her products in a working environment.

- Goldsworthy knew through her prior contacts with design firms that delivery schedules were usually a major source of concern. Using I. A.'s influence, clout, and back channel contacts, she was able to offer a special accelerated delivery schedule to accommodate her three prospective clients and separate her bid from those of her competitors.

Analysis

Goldsworthy took the bull by the horns in developing an identity separate from her boss. She implemented three important steps designed not only to move her away from Tollah's influence but also to distinguish her from the other salespeople:

- *Resources:* She developed the necessary sales tools (brochure and showroom) for her particular specialization. Asking the company to do it would have taken too long, been too expensive, and probably resulted in something less than what she needed to get the job done.

- *Superior involvement:* By flying her prospective customers in for a private meeting, she treated them in a manner consistent with the image she wanted to project. Additionally, she had I. A. involved as well as the senior partner of the company, who was introduced to the prospects. This included them both in her success as well as told the potential customers that they are important.

- *The hook:* Goldsworthy used a hook that her experience told her was important—a favorable delivery schedule. This hook not only helped her get the sale, it also allowed her boss to contribute in a positive way as well by sharing in the effort and the credit.

Goldsworthy's Power Base

Of the three proposals she bid on, she received a contract for one. This contract was both the largest single sale she had ever booked and was geographically the company's most distant customer.

As part of her budding power base, Lisa was fast becoming the department's expert not only in working with interior design firms, but also in shipping and freight companies, raw material suppliers, and the manufacturing division (to meet her special shipping schedules). Because Tollah relied on his personality and old boy network to get him sales, he never developed the channels Lisa sought to nurture. Over the coming months, as Goldsworthy's successes became more frequent, her new channels increased in importance.

Goldsworthy's interaction with her boss changed from one of being adversarial to one of dealing with a peer, albeit one who still carried a chip on his shoulder. Her approach to conversations with I. A. changed to assertive listening. Rarely did she let him babble on about how he would do things. She simply pointed to her improving track record and let her results speak for themselves. Put in terms Tollah could understand, "Money talks and bullshit walks." Yet she never forgot to give Tollah credit where credit was due, especially in front of his three other partners. At the same time, she held him accountable for his actions. As long as she was succeeding she made sure her boss upheld his end of the bargain by not interfering. When he promised to fix manufacturing and delivery problems, she made sure he followed through.

An important part of Lisa's power base was the support she received from her boss. Not only in use of his expertise, contacts, and clout but in his relationship with his peers (who were now becoming Lisa's peers). She fostered Tollah's acceptance with his dependency on her abilities to open a new market for the company's products by keeping him informed of what she was doing, letting him know that her standards of performance were slightly above his, and that she was loyal to him as her boss.

Additionally, she kept his interest in her project by developing two major areas of Tollah's self-interest: (1) I. A. could now move away from just sales management because he was developing a recognized successor with a proven track record and an excellent company-wide image; (2) Lisa's success was due in large part to her boss's perception and judgment of seeing a good idea and going with it.

The Final Push

Many people enjoying the success that Goldsworthy had up to this point would stop short. After all, her boss's most distressing habits had been arrested and her sales were up. For the most part, Tollah left her alone to pursue her own market niche. But by stopping at this point, Lisa would have cured only the symptom rather than the entire disease (Tollahitis). She stuck to her plan to rid her career of him entirely.

Lisa's conquering attack on I. A. Tollah's negative influence came when she seized formal authority to do what she had now been doing in an informal manner for several months. Lisa proposed to the four partners together that a new branch of the sales department be formed specializing in large commercial accounts. Along with her proposal she included a marketing plan, sales estimates, facilities requirements, staffing needs, cost projection, and a profit analysis. She was able to support each of her assumptions with hard data and authoritative research.

In her plan, Goldsworthy would not report to Tollah but would be on the same level. She would have absolute authority over her staff, including hiring, firing, and raises.

By this time, Lisa's sales had eclipsed the other salespeople, and her reputation in the industry was growing. Even Tollah had to admit, she was a dynamo. Goldsworthy was given the position she had created for herself.

Conclusion

The most immediate effect Lisa's success had on her career was to get out from under an incompetent boss who could no more help her career and know what's good for her than he could his own. Additionally, Lisa became the master of her own destiny with regard to rewards, how she spent her time, and in what direction she would take her business. Goldsworthy recognized the need for action and devised a plan to get her where she wanted to go. She found herself working harder than she ever had before but didn't notice because it was herself she was working for rather than someone who could never appreciate it.

She expanded the people who would review her work and appraise her performance to include the other three managing partners. Doing this decreased the prejudice any single partner might attempt to inflict. Additionally, Lisa made sure that her influence and expertise were recognized in the departments that affected her performance like engineering, manufacturing, and shipping. A later part of her plan was to take a hand in designing some of the products to be more conducive to her particular customers and to improve profit margins.

X

Closing Inspirations

Significant changes in our lives never happen easily. It seems as though the most rewarding advances are those that at first appear incredibly risky and difficult to accomplish. Still, the most satisfaction and peace of mind come from knowing that you seized control of your own fate; you managed your promotion; you increased your value and thereby your income; you dictated the way your boss treats you; and, finally, you determined how you will perform your job. With few exceptions, most employers prefer workers who are energetic, creative, and concerned about making the product of their labor, as well as their jobs, the very best they know how. Explosive career advancement awaits those leaders who realize this truth. By submitting to an inept boss, you pass responsibility for your progress and treatment to someone less qualified than you are to know what motivates you and what your goals are.

Lamentably, many bosses out there believe that subordinates will not perform to their expectations, that they will screw up at every opportunity unless they are bullied and battered. We've met several of these tyrannical bosses in the foregoing pages. We've learned how to identify them and how to stop them by using devices such as dependence and dominance. We unearthed how to make Lyan Lobby, the consummate politician, accountable for actions that influence your career. Imagonna Grabontoitz, the disorganized incompetent, can no longer be held responsible for not providing adequate resources, now that you know how to get them yourself. Locomotives like I. B. Meantuu can be made to relinquish the authority you need to avoid being crushed by his heavy-handed manner.

As you encounter these bosses, identify them for what they are and apply the techniques presented to gain control and minimize the risk that an unfit boss has on your career. Like the example of Lisa Goldsworthy, your career probably will not change overnight. Progress will be noticeable, however, as you pass the first hurdle of removing the boss from the pedestal of authority. Imagine the assurance that comes from knowing the boss's temper tantrums do not mean that you are stupid (as he may have even said). Further, you will feel more confident knowing that you have begun the process that will eventually stop the shouting and screaming that comes from so many locomotives and disorganized incompetents.

If you have ever said of your boss, "That guy will drive me crazy," then you have no choice! Fire him! If your boss sees you as a servant who was placed on this earth to further his own career, dump him.

Our jobs are meant to be enjoyed. I have yet to meet a successful person who hated his job or his boss. Those who found either one unsatisfactory changed something to create a situation where they could be successful. The fun you have in your job comes from the way you control what you do. For many, this means creativity. For others, it means freedom to pursue areas that you feel will contribute to profitability. Some people derive satisfaction from controlling the destiny of their company, branch, department, or group. There exists a self-actualized few who have come to grips with their potential and are very happy just being near the seat of power, knowing that they have contributed in some small way to an overall success, without ever being held responsible.

Whatever determines the happiness you derive from your job can be ruined by a maladroit boss if you let him. Don't. In a word, that's the message of this book: Don't. Don't let your boss's problems, inadequacies, and shortcomings become yours. Don't let his or her misery drag you down. Finally, don't let the boss buffalo you into believing he knows what is good for your career and will help you along. He doesn't, and he won't.

I hope you have enjoyed reading this book as much as I have enjoyed writing it.

Best wishes for a healthy, happy career!

Chris Malburg

THE #1 NATIONAL BESTSELLERS—
BE SURE YOU'VE READ THEM BOTH!

The One Minute Manager
and its essential follow-up
Putting The One Minute Manager To Work

__THE ONE MINUTE MANAGER
   Kenneth Blanchard, Ph.D. and Spencer Johnson, M.D.
   0-425-09847-8/$8.50

Whether you manage a multinational corporation or a suburban household, THE ONE MINUTE MANAGER is guaranteed to change your life. Using three easy-to-follow techniques, it shows you how to increase your productivity, save time, and get the most from your job, your family, and yourself...(Large Format)

__PUTTING THE ONE MINUTE MANAGER TO WORK
   Kenneth Blanchard, Ph.D. and Robert Lorber, Ph.D.
   0-425-10425-7/$8.95

This essential follow-up applies the secret of ONE MINUTE GOAL SETTING, ONE MINUTE PRAISINGS and ONE MINUTE REPRIMANDS to REAL-LIFE SITUATIONS...so that you can put them to work in your life immediately! (Large Format)

237